W9-ADG-590

BRUTAL MANDATE

DT714
L6

BRUTAL MANDATE

A JOURNEY TO SOUTH WEST AFRICA

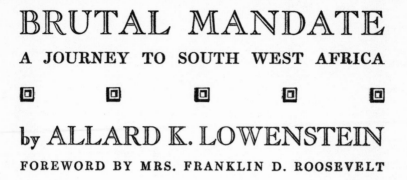

by ALLARD K. LOWENSTEIN

FOREWORD BY MRS. FRANKLIN D. ROOSEVELT

77698

NEW YORK THE MACMILLAN COMPANY 1962

A DIVISION OF THE CROWELL-COLLIER PUBLISHING COMPANY

MACMILLAN NEW YORK, LONDON

1963

FEB

© *Allard K. Lowenstein 1962*

All rights reserved—no part of this book may be reproduced in any form without permission in writing from the publisher, except by a reviewer who wishes to quote brief passages in connection with a review written for inclusion in magazine or newspaper.

Second Printing 1962

The Macmillan Company, New York
Brett-Macmillan Ltd., Galt, Ontario
Macmillan New York, London

Printed in the United States of America

Library of Congress catalog card number: 62-14204

The photograph of Chief Hosea Kutako on the jacket of this book was provided through the kindness of Mr. F. E. McWilliam, the British sculptor.

FOREWORD

BY

Mrs. Franklin D. Roosevelt

How little most of us know about Africa! The other day someone started to tell me something which was a fact about South
Africa but had nothing whatever to do with South West Africa,
which was the area about which we were talking.

This book by Mr. Lowenstein is the story of a trip undertaken to render a service to the people of this mandated
territory. The story itself is told in a natural and completely
fascinating way, with poetic descriptions which give one an
understanding of the country and its people; and the care with
which these young men recorded and documented their findings is a truly remarkable achievement. It required courage,
good judgment, coolness, and persistence.

Mr. Lowenstein and his companions had all of these qualities, but besides they had a depth of human sympathy and
understanding which wiped out the fear of the white man on
the part of the black. Yet through the whole book one can
sense how deep that fear has become. The terror as it is indicated on every page is one of the things any decent white
person will feel shame about.

I have known Mr. Lowenstein for many years. He is a person
of unusual ability and complete integrity. I think he will always
fight crusades because injustice fills him with a sense of rebellion. He wants to be of help in some way, and it must have
been a great satisfaction to him and his companions when the

recordings they had succeeded in smuggling out of South Africa were finally played for members of the Fourth Committee at the United Nations. Their own testimony made a deep impression, so deep that they awakened much new interest in South West Africa and gained new respect for their own country.

I hope this book will be widely read not only in this country but also in many other countries, and my thanks go to Mr. Lowenstein, the author, and to his co-travelers for a remarkable piece of work well done.

BRUTAL MANDATE

At the end of the First World War the victorious Allies, prodded by the President of the United States, decided to undertake a noble experiment in the affairs of nations. The colonies of their recent enemies would not be distributed among the victors. Instead, the interests of the populations indigenous to those colonies would be made the concern of the whole of civilization through the machinery of the new League of Nations. Thus, the indigenous peoples would become wards of the more highly developed nations, to be assisted toward self-government and the various advantages of life in the twentieth century.

To supervise this work, the Mandates Commission of the League of Nations was created, and the administration of each of the former colonies was made the direct responsibility of one of the Allied powers. These responsibilities were described in the Mandate Agreements as "sacred trusts of civilization," and the administering nations agreed to render accounts of their stewardship to the international community through the Mandates Commission.

In practice this high call has worked out remarkably well. Independence has now been achieved or is at hand for all but one of the territories encompassed by the original Mandate Agreements. The exception is a former German colony called South West Africa. Responsibility for administering South West was awarded to Great Britain, which in turn delegated the actual governing authority to the Union of South Africa, then a part of the British Empire.

At the time that the League of Nations was replaced by the United Nations after the Second World War, South Africa had become a sovereign state. Of the Mandatory powers she alone refused to recognize the jurisdiction of the Trusteeship Council as successor to the Mandates Commission. Instead the South African Government announced her intention of incorporating South West into the Union, and to this end ten seats were added to the Union Parliament in 1949 to be filled by the whites of the Territory.

The Union Government maintains that her international obligations in South West expired with the League, a contention that has been rejected repeatedly by the General Assembly and by advisory opinions of the International Court of Justice. In 1953 the United Nations set up a special Committee on South West Africa that issues yearly reports on conditions in the Territory. These reports are based on information collected from statements by petitioners, who the World Court has ruled may submit written or oral evidence, and from such sources as parliamentary debates, codifications of laws, newspaper reports, and official documents and data made public by the South African Government.

South West itself is an area about the size of France and Italy combined, but much of the land is desert or extremely arid, and the population averages less than two per square mile. There are in all just over half a million people, 10 per cent of them white. Of the nonwhite population, 5 per cent are people of mixed blood ("Coloureds"); the rest are members of various African tribal groups, the largest of which are the Ovambos, Hereros, Namas, and Damaras.

The Germans were the first white men to arrive in any numbers, and people of German descent still constitute about one-third of the white population. Virtually all Europeans * and about one-half of the Africans live in the southern four-fifths of the country, which is called the "Police Zone"; to the north are tribal regions that furnish much of the labor force to work the extensive mineral deposits that make South West a rich prize despite the lack of rainfall and the poor quality of the soil.

By the autumn of 1961 the matter of South West Africa's legal position was once again before the Court, this time for a compulsory ruling. Meanwhile it retains its uniqueness as a territory whose status is in dispute between the U.N. and a member state. The sharpness of this dispute has been intensified by the extension of South Africa's apartheid policies to the Territory, and by the contrast with the situation in every other mandated area, and even in those parts of Africa once ruled by colonial powers. For in South West the indigenous population seems further from self-rule than ever.

My introduction to the problem of South West Africa occurred during my first visit to South Africa, at a meeting at the nonwhite Fort Hare University College. My presence had provoked heated denunciations of America's racial attitudes, and I was insisting that the American people do not approve of South Africa's policies—that, in fact, they know nothing about these policies, and do not see how they have any responsibility for them.

This latter remark evoked an angry outcry from a short, dark fellow who had said very little: "You say your people don't see that they are responsible for the things that are done to the black man in South Africa. Well, I come from a place for which your country and the United Nations are directly re-

---

* The terms "European" and "white" are used interchangeably in southern Africa, and are so used in this book; as are the terms "non-European" and "nonwhite."

sponsible, and there things are so much worse that I must come here to get a breath of fresh air."

I assumed this to be a wild overstatement, but no one contested it. His country was of course South West Africa; his name was Jariretundu Kozonguizi. I asked if he could spend a little time telling me about his country. Our "little time" lasted till dawn.

Jariretundu Kozonguizi has since escaped to the United Nations. We have had serious disagreements from time to time about tactical matters and about some of his public statements, but I shall always be grateful to him for his patience that long-ago night when he gave up his sleep to catalogue the plight of his people to an ignorant stranger.

Several weeks later, in the autumn of 1958, I met the Reverend Michael Scott, an Anglican priest who since 1949 has represented several of the tribes of South West Africa at the United Nations. He had just concluded his annual appearance before the United Nations Committee on South West Africa. I knew that Father Scott had gone to South West in 1947 at the request of a number of African chiefs, and that he was an implacable foe of the South African Government; but I was more curious than admiring as I listened to him that day: there were rumors about communist connections, and not a few people referred to him as a crackpot of one sort or another.

Nothing I had heard about Father Scott had prepared me for the remarkable impact of the man. There was a great strength and simplicity to what he said that evoked the deference of diplomats and touched that which makes men want to cheer and weep at once. He was somehow both blunt and gentle, a lean pacifist lion full of a restraining patience and an urgent impatience, as if the two go hand in hand: the patience of a man certain that time would bring victory, an impatience that men do not prod time as much as they could.

When he had finished, a swarm of spectators surrounded

him and followed him down the long corridor. I went to the edge of the group and listened, and found myself thinking that if this man was a crackpot, so were all men who take the burdens of other men as their own.

I read his book *A Time to Speak* and came to know much about his causes, and soon I saw that he makes these causes his life until it is easy to forget that he too must grow weary and discouraged, must on occasion wonder if his will ever be a time to rest. But no hint of such things escapes the gaunt figure in the frayed clerical collar as he dashes about from meeting to meeting, invariably late, often lost, collecting and forgetting briefcases and documents and bits of paper with notes and addresses, doing alone the work that most men would shy from attempting with a staff of half a dozen. Always there is the great patience-impatience, always the people pushing and pulling and seeking this and that; but never is there a show of pique or of self-importance on his part.

By the 1958 session of the General Assembly, Father Scott felt stalemated in his efforts for South West: annexation by the Union seemed headed off, but progress toward trusteeship and freedom was as remote as ever. For several years the United Nations had responded to his pleadings with annual resolutions deploring South African racial policies, the ineffectiveness of which procedure was underscored by South Africa's increasing defiance.

It seemed clear that a major cause of the inertia at the U.N. was the absence of fresh firsthand information from the Territory itself. Michael Scott had not been allowed to return since 1948, and no Africans are allowed to leave. Two Africans —the second my friend Kozonguizi from Fort Hare—had finally managed to make their way to the U.N. with desperate appeals for help, but much of what they said about conditions in South West seemed too wild to believe.

Father Scott and the two Africans were convinced that the

mere gathering and reporting of facts by a disinterested party
could have great value in arousing the conscience of the world,
and that with new evidence much might be done to increase
pressure on the Union to abandon her race policies in South
West or to abandon the Territory itself. Thus had been con-
ceived the idea of an independent trip to South West whose
purpose would be to tape-record statements by tribal chiefs
and other African leaders, photograph living conditions, and
talk with as wide a range as possible of the non-European population. Tapes, pictures, documents, and personal impressions
would then be presented at the U.N.

South African visas are valid for South West, so getting into
the Territory presents no particular problem to white men
who are not on the blacklist of the South African Government.
Once there, however, matters become more complicated, for
it is illegal for Africans to enter "European" areas, and vice
versa, without special passes issued by the government; nor are
such passes likely to be issued to people suspected of planning
to take photographs and conduct interviews for presentation
at the U.N. White strangers would be viewed with suspicion by
an African population more accustomed to white spies than to
white friends, and to come with official approval could hardly
ease such suspicion. More important, to ask for passes would
alert the authorities and thus jeopardize the whole project if
the passes were refused, or if their recipients were provided
with official "guides"; and, in any event, to move about with
the knowledge and permission of the police would be to imperil any Africans who might wish to be critical and to remain
anonymous.

For these reasons, Michael Scott explained, the purpose of
the visit to South West would have to be obscured, and much
of the time there would have to be spent in unauthorized pursuits. Letters of introduction to Africans in various localities

would be provided, and an effort would be made to alert a number of Africans in advance to the impending visit of friends from overseas; but the trip would have to be a hurried one, and would not be without its difficulties.

All this I knew when one day Michael Scott asked me a series of questions so twined about in conditional clauses that I wasn't entirely sure what I had agreed to do for several weeks after I had answered them: Did I think it might be possible to find time to organize a journey to South West to try to obtain firsthand information, if it seemed the time was right and if the necessary arrangements could be made with Africans in the area? Did I feel that finding money might not be an insuperable obstacle, if one put one's efforts to raising some for so urgent a purpose?

I did not feel the obstacles were insuperable, and the idea of such an expedition was exciting to me. I had been active ever since college in various groups opposed to discriminatory practices, and nothing could have interested me more than the possibility of participating in a project that might ease racial injustice.

But the idea of making the trip at the behest of one party to a dispute did trouble me. I agreed it would be necessary to go without seeking the approval of the South African Government, lest frank discussions with Africans be forfeited. But suppose my observations were to differ substantially from the allegations Father Scott and the exiles had been pressing at the U.N.: Would I not then be betraying those who had first proposed the project?

Michael Scott looked surprised: "But we would never want anyone to go whose integrity and objective judgment were the least in doubt," he said. "How could such a trip help? It's the facts we're after, you know."

I think it was then that I made up my mind to do whatever I

could to help gather information about South West Africa, but it seemed doubtful that I could be of much use on a project of this kind without the assistance of resourceful and mechanically skilled people. I set out therefore to find two such people who would be interested in making a trip to South West Africa. The search itself was an interesting experience. Everyone who heard about the expedition seemed to want to help, and a great many volunteered to go.

The motives and personalities of those most eager to go varied considerably. One fellow told me all about an elderly tightfisted aunt who was willing to finance this trip and nothing else; he said I should remember how useful it would be to teach the old lady "the joy of giving." A chap in Indianapolis said this might be his last chance to get out of Indiana. One Ivy League character begged to be included, and then announced he would have to run a check to see if I were a subversive; he said this would take only one phone call, which struck me as being more efficient than the Gestapo at its peak. (I don't know whom he phoned, but I was eventually informed that I was not a subversive.)

The vast majority of those who volunteered were intelligent, idealistic people, many of them quite remarkable in one way or another. I found myself wishing I could take along a whole battalion, including a couple of girls who started out to help find qualified males and ended by deciding they'd like to go themselves. No one who had participated in this quest would have been surprised by the response to the Peace Corps, nor would he doubt the wealth of talent and energy available for such projects.

In the end I was in great luck: I could have searched for years without finding two people who better combined the qualities that were most needed than Sherman Bull of Woodbury, Connecticut, and Emory Bundy of Seattle. There have never been more even-tempered or indomitable companions; they were indispensable in Africa and superb at the U.N. afterward. Africans found their names to be a source of considerable amusement—apparently "Bunny and Bull" sounded like a traveling menagerie—and there was to be a good deal of confusion about which was "the bunny" and which "the bull." Sherman is a wizard with mechanical things, and soon became the uncrowned do-it-yourself king of South West. He is a graduate of Yale who was then in Columbia Medical School and who had been to Africa previously to photograph wild animals. Emory had been president of the student body at the University of Washington, and had considerable experience in primitive areas working on a church project in Yucatan and sailing to remote northwestern islands. He became the expedition's chief note taker, but his greatest contribution was a tireless willingness to do anything that needed to be done.

We read whatever we could find about South West, but it is a far cry from a superficial familiarity to the sort of detailed knowledge we would need to use limited time there wisely. The most optimistic guess was that without the official permits we should have less than two weeks in which to travel about. We should have to know enough about terrain and issues, before we set out, to establish a priority of disputes to probe and to be able to locate significant people and places with a minimum of delay.

At first we feared it would be impossible to acquire so much background about an out-of-the-way place 7,500 miles away, and especially to do so without arousing the curiosity of someone who might tip off the South African Government. But Michael Scott referred us to material compiled by the South West Africa Committee of the U.N., and then the problem was not famine but feast. There were mountains of appeals and petitions that had come from South West itself, the testimony and debates of the Fourth Committee of the General Assembly of the United Nations, the records of the three separate legal proceedings at the World Court in The Hague, and, richest harvest of all, the annual reports of the Committee on South West Africa to the General Assembly.

There were also lengthy discussions with Kozonguizi and Mburumba Kerina, who had been the first African to get to New York from South West; and with Mburumba Kerina's wife, Jane, who is an American. The Kerinas are a remarkable couple who for a number of years had borne the brunt of the year-round effort to keep the issue of South West before the world.

Gradually we acquired a clear idea of which specific grievances and allegations it would be most important to check. We hoped it would be possible to interview leaders of all the tribes, but there was one man we wanted above all others to meet in the Territory. This man was Hosea Kutako, Paramount Chief of the Herero people, then nearly ninety years old, who had become through the years a symbol of courage to Africans of all tribes.

We made plans to leave from New York early in June. No one seemed to think we would achieve much, but the various preparations made good progress until the eleventh hour. Then, suddenly, the last promise of substantial financial help was withdrawn; and on the same day came news that a *New York Times* correspondent had been arrested in South West. The reporter admitted going into the African Location of Windhoek, the capital city, without the necessary police permits. He pleaded guilty, and upon paying a fine was deported. In the aftermath of the arrest came reports of a crackdown on "unauthorized gatherings" inside the Territory.

There were a number of difficult evenings in New York in

late May and early June. I was dubious about the wisdom of Emory's and Sherman's continuing, now that it was impossible to get anything like adequate funds for either of them: Emory had a wife and child to support, and Sherman's financial and other problems had been multiplied tragically by the sudden death of his father six weeks earlier.

Michael Scott had left for the Sahara, but the Kerinas and Kozonguizi said they would understand if we decided the risks were too great to proceed. We agreed that the *New York Times* man had acted properly in his situation, but we also agreed that if we were arrested we could not plead guilty or pay a fine, even if such alternatives were offered to us: to do so would impute a validity to the whole scheme of pass laws that we regarded as illegal violations of the Mandatory Treaty. More than that, it would mean hiding behind an immunity not available to the Africans, who would, after all, be taking far greater risks.

In any event, the Kerinas and Kozonguizi thought it unlikely that we should be given any such option, for most of our offenses would be substantially more serious ones from the point of view of the South African Government. They were convinced, furthermore, that we should be lucky to last one day without being caught; and perhaps for one day the cost was far too high, especially in view of the large sum of money that would now have to be borrowed.

I was troubled most of all by doubts about how much information we should be able to collect before being interrupted. When all is said and done, I remarked one night, even four or five days would be a pitifully inadequate time to spend in so vast a place. "That is so," Mburumba Kerina said, "in the sense that you cannot become an authority on conditions in such a period. But it is not for the purpose of becoming an authority that you are going in the first place. It is to see at

firsthand a state of affairs, and to record interviews and to
look into certain specific matters that you are going. And for
such purposes, even one day can be a long time if it is well
spent. What such a day would mean to people who have been
thirteen years since they last met anyone who cared whether
they lived or died!"

There was a moment when no one spoke, and then Jane
Kerina said: "Sometimes I think the isolation is the worst thing.
It kills hope, and without hope there is nothing."

These statements affected Emory and Sherman much as they
did me. If they were false, it was an outrage that they should
be made. If they were true, how could we refuse to try to bring
hope? And how could anyone know if such statements were
true or false if everyone waited for guarantees of success before they tried to find out?

It was such thoughts as these that confirmed the decision to
go, and it was to such questions as these that we hoped to find
answers in South West. We summarized the general purposes
of the trip in a statement issued in London on the way back
to New York:

"The Government of the Union of South Africa has seen
fit, despite its international obligations, to make it very difficult
to determine the facts of the situation in South West Africa.
It has refused to allow spokesmen for the vast majority of the
people to leave the Territory and present their views at the
United Nations or in other world centers. Further, it has refused to permit the Reverend Michael Scott to return to South
West Africa to consult with the people whose accredited
spokesman he is at the United Nations. It has done everything possible to prevent observers from the U.N. or from
independent organizations interested in the well-being of these
people from traveling freely there. . . .

"Iron curtains are always obnoxious to free men. In a world

grown small and interdependent, they are cancerous. In a territory endowed with international status they are illegal and intolerable. . . . As time passed, it seemed increasingly important that a survey of conditions in South West Africa be undertaken. Allegations by petitioners to the U.N. as well as claims by the Union Government could be weighed more objectively if recent firsthand information were available. . . .

"We spoke with many members of the European minority, and we believe we understand their points of view. Clearly, however, the priority of effort had to be on discussions with non-Europeans, in view of the fact that it is so much more difficult for them to express their feelings to the outside world. We therefore contrived to spend as much time as possible with representatives of the Herero, Nama, Ovambo and others of the indigenous peoples; and we tried to inspect their living conditions, their medical facilities, their educational opportunities, and the extent to which they are free in their own country."

II Mention Africa to most Americans and you evoke blurred images of jungles, savages, and general chaos swarming with intriguing politicians attached to unpronounceable names. Mention South Africa, and you focus on the edge of the blur: the general impression is likely to be of elephants and giraffes circling fields of diamonds while the Mau Mau blow poison darts at helmeted whites.

Until the recent rupture there was a vague sense that South Africa had something to do with the British Empire. In at least one western city antiapartheid pickets who could find no listing for "South Africa" in the local telephone directory are reported to have demonstrated in front of the British Consulate instead. No doubt this irritated the British officials, and in any case it was unfair. South Africa has been master of her own doings and undoings ever since the Statute of Westminster became law in 1931, and the British are not responsible for the apartheid laws, at least not in the sense the picketers thought.

Moreover there are no Mau Mau in South Africa, an absence which the South African Government likes to reiterate, as if thereby guaranteeing tourists against racial unpleasantness if they will visit the Union. But there are factors present that one day soon may make the Mau Mau troubles in Kenya seem a squall before the monsoon season.

The Union of South Africa has been in existence since 1910. From that time until May 31, 1961, she formed part first of the British Empire and then of the Commonwealth. In

1961, in response to the wishes of 52 per cent of the white voters and as a result of discussions at the gathering of Commonwealth prime ministers in London, a President replaced the Queen as head of the nation, membership in the Commonwealth was terminated, and the Union of South Africa became officially the "Republic of South Africa." *

The country itself is a historical accident, the unruly offspring of a liaison between nature at her most voluptuous and mankind at his most discordant. Nowhere are greater natural riches and more dissimilar groups of people contained in a place of comparable size.

The territory of South Africa is 472,494 sq. miles, one-seventh that of the continental United States. But the statistic is misleading, for a large part of the land is too poor to support much habitation. The total population is less than 15,000,000, about 9 per cent of the figure for the United States, and of that total about two-fifths cluster around half a dozen urban areas. There are 10,000,000 black people ("Africans"), 1,400,000 mulattoes ("Coloureds"), 500,000 Indians, and 3,000,000 whites. Nor do these overall categories describe homogeneous or united groups: the tensions within as well as among them, especially in the great metropolitan centers, are ferocious and are not decreasing.

The European community has two major components, each of which was in general control of two of the four political units that combined to form South Africa. Two of these units, Natal and the Cape of Good Hope, had been British colonies; the others, Orange Free State and the Transvaal, had been independent republics whose whites were largely of Dutch and Huguenot descent.

---

* In this work, out of habit and to avoid heightening confusion, we shall speak of South Africa as "the Union" whether the reference is pre- or post-Republican.

It was this latter group, now known as Afrikaners but once called "Boers" (an Afrikaans word meaning "farmers"), who fought an ingenious and almost interminable war against the English-speaking colonies, and indeed against the British Empire itself, at the turn of the century. The republics surrendered after three bitter years that provided the first harbingers of some of the horrors into which modern warfare would devolve. And although the terms of peace were generous and brought Boer and Briton together as equals in a new Union within the British Empire, the hatreds loosed from scorched earth and concentration camps were formidable enough to envenom relations between the two groups through the decades since. Nor is the end yet in sight.

Not the least remarkable aspect of the Boer War, and perhaps one of the most prophetic, was the fact that the vast majority of the people who lived in the contested areas had virtually no part in the proceedings and very little stake in the result. In Rayne Kruger's words: "The Boers said the war was for liberty. The British said it was for equality. The majority of the inhabitants, who were not white at all, gained neither liberty nor equality."

What the Boers lost in the war they more than regained after the Act of Union, thanks to the dictates of the British conscience and the workings of biology. The enemy restored their franchise, their fecundity gave them a majority; and sixty years after the surrender they were masters of a new republic that included the old British colonies as well as their own former territory. So now it is the turn of the million and a quarter English-speaking South Africans to brood and grumble while triumphant Afrikaners preach the virtues of white unity.

Despite historical and cultural antipathies, both sections of the European community live extremely well, enjoying the bounty of an economy based on lavish supplies of cheap labor and precious minerals. Meanwhile, the three-quarters of the population that is not white, and that supplies the cheap labor, stews and festers in a wretched poverty that is aggravated by the interwoven presence of such great wealth, and is made almost unbearable by a statutory straitjacket that strangles all hope of escape. For here, by law as well as by custom, the best of everything is to be reserved for whites and the worst for blacks, who are always to be low stripe on the zebra regardless of personal ability, individual effort, or communal virtue.

With fanatic thoroughness the government goes about the task of codifying racial stratifications that will make permanent the economic and other disparities. Here in the name of "separate development" the government determines everything about everyone by his race—and determines as well what that race is; the undertaking is of an enormity that dwarfs even the Nuremberg decrees. Once a man has been investigated and categorized as "white," "black," or "other," the government tells him where he may live, what kinds of jobs he may hold, what schools he may attend and what he will be taught there, if and where he may travel, whom he may marry or sleep with, and what, if any, political rights he is to have.

Nor is there to be any nonsense about equality in the separated facilities. With exceptions so trivial and so theoretical that to recite them is to illustrate the harshness of the discrimination, the black man is not allowed to rise above the most menial kinds of labor, or to own his own land, or to earn a living wage, or to obtain a decent education, or to vote, or to walk on the streets of a city without first obtaining permission from white officials. He is, furthermore, always subject to the caprices of the head of the South African Government who, by statutory enactment, is the "Supreme Chief" of every African.

The government has made one concession to world opinion outraged by such laws; and this concession is not in the nature of the laws but in the explanation of their purpose. Now *apartheid* (separate development), not *baasskap* (white supremacy), is the official justification; and what is said about apartheid to win votes at home is not what is said about it to win friends abroad. For the official position now is that the black man is to have his own areas (*Bantustans*), and there his rights shall be as the white man's are in his; so the black man is a guest when he is in an area belonging to the white man, and a guest has no rights except such as may be given to him by the government of the place in which he is visiting. And the black man is always a guest in the areas that belong to the white man, even if he has lived in the same place since birth and knows no other home.

This is the doctrinal heart of apartheid: the physical separation of each racial group so it may develop "in its own way"—what that way is, of course, to be determined by the government chosen by the white electorate. The white man will determine which areas belong to which race (82 per cent for himself, 13.7 per cent for the Africans, 4.3 per cent for everyone else) and will determine when the black man is ready to run his own affairs, even in areas that have been designated black areas. But if anyone doubts the equity of such an arrangement, or notes that its consequences to the black man are not distinguishable from the consequences of baasskap, that man must be an enemy of the Afrikaner people, of South Africa, of white Christian civilization itself.

Whatever the merits of the Bantustans in theory, two-thirds of the Africans work directly for the white man, one-third on his farms and one-third in his mines and cities. They are likely to continue as this strange sort of guest for the foreseeable future, for the lavish white economy depends on their presence.

The remaining third are the celebrated tribal Africans, jammed and starving in the generally inferior land set aside as Reserves. Apartheid theorists used to insist that all Africans would have to "return" to a Reserve whether they had ever seen one or not, a procedure that would have whatever merit may lie in the fact that it would be equally disastrous for both races. There is progressively less talk in South Africa of this final solution as its implications become clearer to the European electorate. But with the modification that all Africans will be "free" to "return" to a Reserve if not content with life as guests in a white area, it remains an important part of the government's information efforts overseas.

Somewhere in a confused, neither black nor white middle flounder the Coloureds, centered in the Cape, and the Indians, centered in Natal. With miniscule exceptions, they have no more political rights than Africans, but their poverty is not so grinding. They are allowed to seek better-paying positions under the provisions of the Job Reservations Act, and a modest number of business and professional people even provide some middle-class leaven.

Most important, neither Coloureds nor Indians are required to carry the passbooks that are the most hated symbol and instrument of the oppression of the Africans by the whites (although Indians may not travel between provinces without a special pass). Virtually all African males over the age of fourteen must carry one of these books. A few "exemptions" have been granted, and a pass is solemnly issued to certify that the bearer is exempted from carrying a passbook; but he had better have this strangest pass of all, the pass that says he need not have a pass, on his person at all times.

The government explains these books as a measure necessary to control the influx of blacks to the cities. Without one

properly endorsed by various authorities, it is illegal to stay
more than seventy-two hours in an urban area, or to seek
employment, or to travel to the next town, or to live with
relatives other than a wife and minor children. There are
even situations in which it is illegal for a husband and wife
to live together without special permission. And without individual dispensations granted by appropriate whites, no African
may be on the streets of a town after curfew (usually 9:00
P.M.) or be absent from work or quit a job.

Thus the pass laws put the African at the mercy of his
employer as well as that of the police. If he is fired, his right
to stay in his house is terminated; if he has not found a new
job within a week (after securing the necessary permit to look
for one) he is subject to arrest for a pass that is not in order,
or to banishment to a Reserve in which he may know no one
and have no way to earn a living. There are other sections
in the books: they must be stamped periodically, for example,
to show that tax payments are up to date. Moreover, an
African whose pass is in order but who is caught without it is
as great a criminal as one who has no pass at all. Paddy
wagons roam the streets of cities and police raid Locations
house to house to check passes.

The total effect is a morass of such complex regulations enforced so harshly that no African can ever feel safe from arrest. Professor Julius Lewin of the University of the Witwatersrand in Johannesburg concluded after a study that any African
can be arrested at any time and "any competent prosecutor
will have no difficulty whatever in finding some offense with
which he could be charged." More than one thousand Africans
are convicted every *day* of some pass law violation; and more
than a *million and a quarter* are detained every year by the
police for one irregularity or another.

Nor is arrest for such offenses a matter to be taken lightly.

Beatings by the police are commonplace, convictions routine, fines heavy; and a man may end up in a jail much like a sewer, or doing prison-farm labor for six months. Such a man is lucky if he can get word to his family so they may know that he has not vanished into thin air. By the time he has served out his sentence he will have lost his job, and with it the right to live in his house or anywhere in an urban area; and so he will have to start all over again with the seeking of a permit to seek work, which may not be granted because he is now an ex-convict. The passes are now being extended to include African women.

It was against these pass laws that the protest meetings were called that culminated in the killings at Sharpeville on March 21, 1960. The government has subsequently announced that it will enforce these laws more vigorously in the future. This sort of response is characteristic of its reaction to each new sign of unrest; and it is this sort of response that strikes many disinterested observers as hardly short of lunacy.

In the name of self-preservation, the government speeds the alienation of buffer racial groups by depriving them of token political representation and threatening to evict them from homes and businesses developed over a century. It further embitters the tiny group of nonwhite intellectuals who manage to emerge by depriving them of access to first-rate universities and reminding them in every possible way that no matter what their talents, they can never escape an inferior status; it excites the passions of long-quiescent Africans in unsophisticated Reserves by inflicting upon them chiefs subservient to the state and then shooting up tribal groups that object; it even contrives to multiply mistrust and division within the European minority by pursuing sentimental vendettas against irrelevant symbolisms (the Queen, the Union Jack, the British Anthem) cherished by the 40 per cent who are English-speaking.

All this is done to a great clatter of pronouncements revealing future horrors yet to be uncorked, and dismissing those who oppose the proceedings as communists. And it is accompanied by bannings, jailings, shootings, and whippings on a scale that would make Franco or Castro blush. Indeed, it would not be easy to distinguish the political rights of South Africans from those of citizens of the Soviet Union, except that the wording of the laws of the Soviet Union is designed to preserve the pretense of freedom, while in South Africa the stolid integrity of the courts has forced the government to enact into law each new authorization to trespass.

But because South Africa has no constitution in the American sense, no Bill of Rights that can be sustained by courts against legislative or executive assault, the courts can provide no lasting protection against a majority in Parliament determined to do as it pleases. And the Nationalist Government, despite its failure to obtain the support of a clear majority even of Europeans, does exactly as it pleases. Its special wrath is reserved for the hardy handful of Europeans who join with non-Europeans in nonviolent efforts to bring about a nonracial society. These are traitors who must be incarcerated in endless trials, or deported, or whisked into the night by the secret police to disappear for three or four months without warrants, bail, or subsequent explanations. (The government greets protests about such procedures either by denying they exist or by pluming itself for its efficiency in curbing communists.)

Thus opposition groups must try to function under ground rules that are changed at any time at the whim of the government. If a few white men representing Africans in Parliament become a nuisance, their seats are abolished. If the technique of nonviolent protest campaigns gains momentum, it is made a crime to "commit an offence by way of protest against any law, or in support of any campaign for the repeal or modification of any law." If a man becomes too effective an opponent of the established order, he is deported or jailed without charges or exiled to a remote village and prohibited from attending meetings.

The powers for suppression now vested in and used by the government make it impossible for dissenters to know what they may safely say or do, or when or how they have crossed the line of what is tolerated. Newspapers may be suspended, organizations outlawed, individuals prohibited from traveling within or without the Union, dwellings and offices searched at any time without notice or warrant. Special permission must be obtained for most meetings at which ten or more Africans are to be present, and *any* meeting may be broken up—even a meeting in a private house—if a police official decides that an offense against some law may be committed or planned at the meeting in question.

Furthermore, there is an official called the "Liquidator" who can "name" anyone as a communist. There is no appeal, and the Liquidator need offer no evidence to support his action. A person so named becomes a political leper who may not make speeches or attend meetings, and who may be removed by fiat from his home, banished to some distant point, and prevented from entering any other area. In view of the consequences of being so named, and of the government's lavish use of the word in describing those who differ with it, the statutory definition of "communist" may be of some interest: "A communist is a person who professes to be a communist or who . . . is deemed by the Governor-General or, in the case of an inhabitant of the territory of South West Africa, by the Administrator of the said Territory, to be a communist on the ground that he is advocating, advising, defending or encouraging or had at any time after the date of commencement of this Act advocated, advised, defended or encouraged the achievement of *any of the objects of communism* or any act or *omission* which is calculated to further the achievement of any such object." (Author's italics.)

Nor need the Cabinet await legislative authorization to make new laws, for Parliament has granted it authority to proclaim a state of emergency in given areas or throughout the country. Once this has been done, it can rule by decree for as long as it chooses to do so. There is therefore virtually no political activity which by fiat or specific statute the government cannot control. Not only can it do these things; it does them regularly. The two leading African political organizations—both pledged to nonviolence and both urging a nonracial democracy in South Africa—have been banned, as have countless individuals. More than two thousand people of all races were detained for varying periods after Sharpeville, most of whom were eventually released without ever being charged with anything. More than ten thousand disappeared in the period preceding the celebration attendant upon the establishment of the Republic.

This is South Africa in the seventh decade of the twentieth century. Strangest of all, the government that perpetrates all this complains bitterly that it is misunderstood or misrepresented by anyone who reports its own laws or repeats abroad what its leaders say at home. It is as though Hitler had insisted that his policies were for the good of non-Aryans, and had denounced the National Conference of Christians and Jews for not rewarding his efforts with a testimonial dinner.

We arrived in Leopoldville on June 17th, and spent most of that night cramming and copying from U.N. documents. Then we shed the documents and inscribed on a road map whatever names and data seemed likely to be necessary in South West Africa. This map we then tucked away, together with such material as the letters of introduction from Kerina and

Kozonguizi, in places we thought unlikely to be searched by South African Customs.

The next morning dawned muggy and bleak, and we dozed on the plane during the long descent to Johannesburg. We wondered if a last-minute leak, coupled perhaps with the presence of the tape recorder on Sherman's shoulder, might stir suspicions; and wondered if we had chosen wisely the places where we had concealed things, or if perhaps we had bitten off more than we could chew. While we were still wondering about such things we were at Jan Smuts Airport and safely through Customs, unsearched and unharassed, but unsure what to do first in this extraordinary metropolis that is the brain and pocketbook of South Africa and the hub of the greatest industrial complex in the Southern Hemisphere.

Here we would try to find a vehicle and prepare ourselves as best we could for the expedition. Many people were eager to help in any way they could, but nothing anyone else might do could change the habits and values that had been ingrained by middle-class American backgrounds and that are not always assets in a police state. At times it was a handicap to be inexperienced with tapped wires and illegal meetings, but the more general problem was when and how loudly to speak up. Often it would have been wiser to have had a less spontaneous indignation, and we never managed to rid ourselves of distaste for the duplicity frequently required to get information or to get into prohibited areas.

Of all the freedoms South Africa lacks, the most universal is the freedom from fear, for here almost everyone is afraid of someone else, and usually with good cause. This is a country of subterfuges and repressed reactions, of human intercourse inhibited and circumscribed until the calculated gesture becomes an ordinary posture and men think it natural to behave as if they were forever onstage.

Packs of African hoodlums (*tsotsis*) terrorize urban areas with impartial indifference to the race of their victims. The government, as we have noted, performs a similar function for its opponents, whose phone calls and mail are intercepted and who may vanish at any moment to spend unexplained days or weeks unnoticed in an unknown cell.

Then there are the white men who have no worry that their phones are tapped but who sleep with guns under their pillows and locked gates at the top of their stairways; this one may be worth a million pounds and that one may sit in Parliament or at the head of his profession, but their wives tremble when the servants huddle. Do not be surprised if such men take you aside to inquire of prospects for starting over again in America or Britain or Canada or Israel.

The greatest fears of all are the fears of the white man for the black and of the black man for the white. The fear of the white man is that he will be swamped and his civilization drowned in a sea of blacks. So strong is this fear that it has already overwhelmed some of his noblest traditions and undermined some of the finest contributions of the civilization he hopes to preserve.

The fear of the black man is less theoretical, an omnipresence more personal and perhaps more rational, since it is rooted in long experience and in the existing legal code of the country, and is reinforced by a hundred daily encounters and a thousand permanent contrasts which do as much to poison the atmosphere as the law itself.

Perhaps the worst thing about these crossed fears is that each feeds on the other until communication is never free of them and becomes a funnel of misunderstandings that further nourish them. Thus the black man retreats into a constant groveling, and the white man sees him only in the mask of cloying deference that he has forced him to wear, hears him only through the endless staccato of "sir" and "baas" that brings subservience to each sentence, knows him only as feudal lord knew faceless serf.

The cleverest black man is the one who learns to lie most convincingly to the white, the one who remembers that the master wants to hear only what he wants to hear, and who knows that he wants to hear even that in tones purged of spirit and of any hint of independence. And when most black men accommodate to such a tone, the few who speak with candor must appear to the white not as men of unusual integrity, but as agitators: misleading, inciting, dangerous, wicked; and theirs shall be the fate of the bad example.

Such are the customs of the place that minor matters can irritate or upset the newcomer quite out of proportion. The African who insists on calling you "sir" because "It is a bad habit to get out of, sir"; the post-office window for blacks where the old lady waits endlessly while the separate line of Europeans is served, replenished, and served again; the stuttering terror of the African service station attendant who discovers while putting gasoline in a car that the gas cap is missing, and knows his employer will accuse him of stealing it and perhaps fire him if the driver of the car complains. One wonders if it is possible to get used to such things; it is essential to get them in perspective if one is to keep functioning in South Africa.

My best lesson about this matter of perspective came one evening in Johannesburg while I was meeting with Oliver Tambo, Deputy President of the African National Congress and one of South Africa's most distinguished citizens. All at once we realized we were both late—I for a meeting at a far end of town, he to make the last train to the Location where he lived. Interracial taxi riding is illegal, and it was impossible to find a cab that would accept Oliver as a passenger. There was nothing for him to do but start running, laden with groceries and briefcase, toward the station perhaps a mile away.

It was unthinkable to ride in a cab in such a situation, and I sputtered along, fuming and vowing vengeance. Oliver, however, was very calm. He told me I was a fool to let something so trivial upset me.

"Come now, man," he said as we trotted, "we would go crazy if such things got to us. Think of the jailings and beatings and people starving, and see this little nothing for what it is, or you'll be useless in a week. And," he added, "take the next taxi you can get—there's no sense to both of us missing our meetings."

It is the frank purpose of the law to prevent interracial associations, and it is illegal for black and white to do together most of the things that friends ordinarily wish to do.

That any friendships survive the enormous legal and psychological obstacles is testimonial to the durability of human affection; and many have survived, especially among younger people who used to meet at the two great English-speaking universities, Cape Town and Witwatersrand ("Wits"), which the government has now closed to nonwhite students.

Warm relationships between employers and long-time African servants are not infrequent, but these are circumscribed both by the usual limitations of such relationships and by the unique stresses of life in South Africa. Fashionable Johannesburg has tried for years to laugh at the story of the kindly housewife who asked her devoted black cook if in a "showdown" she would really kill the family of which she was virtually a part. "Oh, no, Missie," the cook is supposed to have replied, "I kill the family next door, cook next door kill you."

Fear and suspicion and prejudice also envelop and undercut

contacts between English and Afrikaner, to say nothing of those between English or Afrikaner and Jew, and between supporters of the government and its opponents.

It is one thing in a free country to preserve friendships despite political disagreements; it is quite another to try to ignore politics in a country where disagreement and "treason" can be synonymous, and where Christianity to one man is communism to the next. Here everyone is sorted out by racial and ethnic groupings, and then boxed off and hedged around by problems of trust and viewpoint. To sustain warm ties with people whom one regards as traitors, or even as potential traitors, is not easy; and fear of group or government disapproval further impedes such associations.

All the jolly hoopla stirred up by various goodwill societies has failed to produce any significant break in the ancient barriers between the European communities. Even the considerable intermarrying that has gone on has bred more children who have been absorbed by one community or the other than children who are at home in both.

This is the result partly of the snobbishness of many English-speaking South Africans, and partly of the peculiar defensive tribal attitudes encouraged by many Afrikaners whose fierce inward loyalties make those not of the *Volk,* or worse yet those strayed from the Volk, not fully trustworthy, whether in government service or as friends. When loyalty to this view of an Afrikaner mystique is made the test of affection or of loyalty to South Africa, few who are not Afrikaner Nationalists can or would wish to pass it.

Sherman, Emory, and I were always frank about our point of view on current affairs. We made a habit of telling ardent supporters of the government that our friendship was not contingent on political agreement, but that if theirs was it would be best to understand right away how we felt. Our hosts then could determine the nature of our association; most of the time a pleasant relationship survived. I suspect that our activities in South West Africa and at the U.N. have changed this, and that we have now left the permissible category of uninformed foreign critics to become enemies of the Afrikaner nation. In the face of this, the abandonment of individual friendships is a minor sacrifice for the ardent Afrikaner.

In fact, so great is the pressure toward solidarity that few Nationalists would maintain close ties with someone deemed an enemy of the Volk. But many of the South Africans whose friendship I cherish most are Afrikaner Nationalists, and it saddens me to think that these friendships may have been sundered by our differences in viewpoint; it would sadden me more if I thought my Afrikaner friends really believed me to be their enemy. They must know privately that this is not so, and that few visitors have been more captivated or have left South Africa more eager to help in any way possible to salvage what is great about these remarkable people.

And there is much that *is* remarkable about these Afrikaner people, hardy and undaunted in their isolation. But there is much that is tragic and wrongheaded about them too, and it is a false friend who mouths uncritical praise, knowing that such gentle hypocrisies encourage delusions that must in due course destroy the group he is praising. I came to feel that it was important to avoid leaving any implication that affection denotes conversion, or that seeing Afrikaners means believing in Afrikaner policies. It was not always easy to do this without abandoning good manners.

I shall long remember a dinner that came at the end of a visit at an Afrikaans university. It had been a delightful visit at the finest moment of the southern African winter, the afternoons crisp in slanting sunlight that invited hookey and made long shadows early, the evenings chill and soaring under a moon that insisted its way through leaves and windows. We strolled through modern classrooms, drank American-style milkshakes, and sprawled on pleasant malls green despite the season, peaceful oases among the lively hostels where hundreds of undergraduates studied and ate and slept and carried on in the way of the robust and carefree.

Two nights in a row we had become so involved in vigorous discussions with large groups of students that sleep had been all but forgotten. I was surprised to find that candid airings of South Africa's racial situation are rare at Pretoria, Stellenbosch, and other Afrikaner universities, and gratified that ours were so uninhibited and welcome once under way.

In addition to politics there had been a lot of the good-natured fun that is common to any large coeducational gathering of the young and healthy: pep rallies, songfests, athletic competitions, social affairs, and so on and on. Sometimes it was hard to remember that this was not Ames, Iowa, or Norman, Oklahoma; that it was, indeed, barely five miles from another universe where misery seethed and where these smiling young faces were symbols of all that made life unbearable.

I could never forget that other world. It haunted my enjoyment of songfests and all the rest, as it had in lesser measure during the lovely days at Chapel Hill; and left me feeling vague guilts such as men must have felt in the 1930's who had delightful German friends given to spitting at Jews when not at friendly sporting events.

And yet these were good people, lovable and human, and I rationalized being there by hoping there was some value in speaking old truths to new ears, some value in seeking for words that might penetrate this illusory nirvana before it was too late for these good and human people and those five miles away to discover each other.

And now the guest from overseas, charmed by the unaffected warmth of his hosts and grateful for so abounding a hospitality, was at dinner for the last time; and presently, amidst a considerable nostalgia, the chairman said generous and graceful things. I knew I should have to respond, and should be as generous and graceful as I could in return; and I was torn between the duty to speak frankly on the one hand, and feelings of affection and gratitude on the other.

Then I heard the chairman saying, "We all know our good friend came here, as do so many from overseas where the press tells so many lies about us, with many false ideas about us and our country; and we are grateful that he has taken the time to see us as we are, and that he will leave here understanding us and ready to correct those lies whenever he comes across them from now on."

The room was full of gladness for the new alliance with an understanding America, and I knew through the cheering that affection and gratitude were no longer on the other hand from duty, for it would be only cowardly, not affectionate or grateful, to let such an impression stand. There were more cheers, and people were singing "For He's a Jolly Good Fellow," and then I was standing and trying to figure out how to say what had to be said.

I managed first some words of gratitude, which made it no easier to proceed.

"You are quite right"—it was my voice, but it seemed somehow to be functioning independently—"that I had been misled about what I would find in South Africa. I came expecting to find a group of Nazis pursuing such mad racial policies that they were going to be pushed into the sea, and I expected to be glad that they were going to be pushed into the sea. Instead I have found some of the most generous and wonderful people I have ever met. I have felt more at home with you than at any other place outside my own country; this has become, in some magic way, my country too."

I paused, and hoped someone would make a nosie somewhere; but there was only silence.

"These are very different things from what I had expected— this deep affection, this feeling of somehow being part of your country. And, feeling these things, I cannot be glad that you are pursuing such mad racial policies that you are going to be pushed into the sea, and that no one will help you then because you will have brought it all on yourselves."

It was easier after that; in all I must have talked—blunt, emotional things—for twenty minutes or more. Then there were questions, and speeches in the guise of questions, and speeches in the guise of answers, for yet another hour.

Afterward there were many who stayed to talk still more; and many who knew affection was what had made me speak out, and some who said they were grateful that there was a friend who had been candid and that such things had not been said to them before.

A few hours of frank talk convert no one, but I think such moments are useful because they can arouse and reinforce the grave doubts that lie dormant beneath the façade of monolithic Afrikaner unity. I do not credit these doubts very much to an awakening conscience, much as I should prefer that to be their source, but rather to a native common sense now beginning to find an unexpected ally in that very instinct for self-preservation which has so often supplied the excuse for treading on other groups.

No substantial segment of the Afrikaner community has yet hinted publicly at such a wobbling; but in his secret places how much of each individual now wavers—20 per cent? 25 per cent? And how much does each blunt warning, each new

boycott announcement, each refusal to seat apartheid delegations at world meetings—how much does each added drop of
isolation or censure add to the inner wavering? At what point
will these pressures have mounted sufficiently to cause large
numbers of Afrikaners to revolt against the tribal chant that
defies their own inner judgment?

If the pressures from the noncommunist world do not build
up swiftly—if the present Afrikaner leadership can talk its way
out of quarantine—the Volk is doomed. Each sign of outside
approval delays the acceptance by rational Afrikaners of the
inevitability of change; and there is no time for further delay.
For if change is not gradual and cooperative it will be sudden
and violent; and if it is not induced with help from the
West it will be wrought with help from elsewhere, from places
less scrupulous about human life, less attuned to Gandhi and
Christ. Then it will be too late to save white South Africa and
the considerable contributions it could make to Africa and to
centuries still to come.

There are many to whom this concern for the future of the
present masters is second only to concern for the present
victims in spurring on efforts to influence the course of events
in South Africa.

A different kind of dilemma troubled us when we were
guests of people opposed to the Nationalist Government but
equally opposed to liberal "agitation."

Most English-speaking South Africans fit this description.
Some are deliberately nonpolitical; many are so content with
the adornments of white supremacy that anyone supporting
"nonracialism" must seem a traitor to something far higher
than Nationalist rule: to South Africa itself, or, even worse,
to the white race.

All in all, these are cultivated and charming people. The

well-to-do among them are a numerous and delightful set, devotees of the arts, commuters to the Continent, gentry used to the best of everything: sporting to opponents, generous to guests, kind to inferiors, loyal to a high sense of honor. If their political attitudes are nineteenth century, their social consciences are not quite so, and they are not entirely unaware of the incongruity between what is and what ought to be.

But by and large the older people are too committed and too comfortable to speak out. And so there frequently arises one of those painful gaps that result when the younger generation is right and cannot be ignored or converted, and the older is too contented and cautious to swing itself around to where it suspects it ought to be. Thus many of the children of the segregationist United party say "mister" to non-Europeans, and visit in African homes, and wish to have Africans visit in their homes; and some become Progressives or Liberals or even worse. But there is more to life than politics even in South Africa, and families go on together and tussle over or resign themselves to the gap, as temperament and circumstance may decree.

Then into the mansions of their parents, with their broken-glass ledges on the high walls to keep out marauding natives, the heirs and heiresses bring three visitors from afar whose nonracial sentiments are as echoes of their own. But it is the graciousness of Anglo-Saxon tradition that each man's views are his own, and hospitality is lavish despite politics. Perhaps there is even the resounding of an unacknowledged chord of agreement somewhere in a distant tired conscience.

All of which was fine when that was all there was to it; but sometimes the visitors at least knew it was not. Then it was the turn of *our* consciences to boggle, for our presence had turned our hosts into unwitting providers of a base from which to plan the smuggling of someone out of the Union or the holding of clandestine meetings with non-European leaders—arrangements that could cause unpleasantness for gracious folk who were innocent bystanders.

As a rule, our hosts knew our viewpoint but nothing of these activities. I hope nothing we did was retroactively attributed to any of them, to their embarrassment or discomfiture. It was never our intention to bring trouble to people who have not taken sides, or rather to people who are not aware that they have taken sides by staying neutral. Indeed, the possibility of reprisals against those who were kind to us often inhibited us from accepting invitations to stay where convenience dictated.

Despite these scruples there were times when we found ourselves willy-nilly in situations that could have been awkward for our hosts had we been caught. What to do then became the quintessence of conflicting loyalties: the possible risk to gracious bystanders had to be measured against possible additional risks to trusting nonwhites and to the plans for South West. I was tempted under such circumstances to tell the younger people who had invited us what we were about, but this seemed cowardly as well as dangerous. At best it would implicate them much more deeply in our affairs for not reporting us to the authorities; at worst it could mean betrayal of more than just the immediate project.

Only once did I resort to such a step, and then not entirely voluntarily. I had become involved unexpectedly in an undertaking that entailed a good deal of coming and going, much of it at unusual hours. When cryptic phone messages began arriving, I said fulsome thank-yous and announced I was leaving.

The young lady responsible for my presence smelled a rat. She had been far too helpful not to have guessed something was afoot, and her sense of adventure as well as her distaste for the government was aroused. She lured me out to dinner at

her club, and there in candlelight and to soft music she hinted
and asked gentle prying questions. We fenced a while, and
then suddenly, in the middle of a slow dance, she smiled at
me and said: "I know why you're moving out. You don't want
to involve us in what you're up to. But I know what you're up
to, and I'm already involved."

If this was an evening with Mata Hari, I was enjoying all
of it; but I could not believe it was anything of the sort. For
this was not merely a beautiful girl but a generous one whose
loyalty and courage had already been demonstrated on half a
dozen occasions when her car had turned up unsummoned
or her quick wit had covered an awkward lapse on an overheard phone call. I must have realized long since that she
could not have been so helpful if she had not had some notion
of what was going on.

So I told her the situation, and it turned out there was
much about it that she had not guessed; still she insisted I was
not to move out. "Without the house you're baseless, and without my car you're immobilized, and I can't very well trail you
around the countryside if I first have to hunt you up several
times a day. Whatever would the neighbors think?"

"The neighbors" are as pressing a concern in the plushness
of South African suburbs as they were to barons in medieval
France, and we both knew for "neighbors" to read "parents."
So I said: "That's just the point. It's simply not fair for me to
stay on."

"You'd make a hell of a spy," she said, "worrying about
what's fair to strangers while your mission gets shot to pieces."
And her eyes laughed an accusation we both knew was true:
without her help it would be almost impossible to achieve what
I had set out to do. But these were hardly "strangers" I was
concerned about—to her far less than to me.

So we haggled through an evening, lovely in many ways

and strange in so many others; but when all was said and done it was clear to me that I could not stay on unless her parents knew what I was doing and invited me to stay on anyway. And I could not take the chance of sharing such information with respectable well-fixed people of ancient South African loyalties, no matter how hospitable they might be, and no matter how helpful their daughter. The circle, if not precisely vicious, was at any rate inescapable. I would have to go.

It grew late, and I had suggested we ought to be heading home when all at once she announced a solution: "I shall tell my parents, and there can be no additional risk because I shall tell them I'm in it all the way, and if they say a word to the authorities they must turn me in too."

It was, after a fashion, indeed a solution. Blackmail, I called it, and she knew she had won; though in a real sense, of course, it was I who was the winner. But by morning, away from the charms of my co-conspirator, I decided I could not go through with it, and began to pack.

Suddenly there rang out across the courtyard the booming voice of the lady of the house calling my name. I walked out to the yard feeling almost as relieved as tense—at least the whole thing would be over quickly. Mother and daughter were standing side by side.

"I was just packing," I said.

"Packing? What rubbish! We've just agreed you must stay on. Such a good tennis player. Very handy to have around." She stopped. Then she smiled. "Don't be clumsy about it, will you? And here—you'll be needing this, you bloody fool. It's from an anonymous admirer." And she put £10 in my pocket.

We were not organizing rebellion or filching secret papers or distributing weapons. None of our activities would have been illegal in a free country, or indeed in a country not gone mad. For that matter, none of them would have been necessary.

Even in the context of South Africa, relatively little of what we did was illegal in itself, but such distinctions are lost once you have jumped into what the government has called the "polluted stream" of nonwhite politics. Then attending the least political of functions can become adequate excuse for official retribution if Africans are present. And the uncertainty of what is permissible and what will arouse police suspicions has created an atmosphere of caution and fear among Europeans that sometimes is excessive but is always inhibiting.

The degree to which this political fear penetrates the lives of white people varies greatly. I remember arriving in a sophisticated Afrikaner home early on my first visit in the Union to find a group of people in earnest quest for ways "to bring the country back to its senses." At the time I felt as if I had stumbled into a Bonds for Israel rally at the Nile Hilton. Later I realized it is safer for well-to-do Afrikaners to criticize apartheid than for anyone else, provided they are prepared for a degree of abuse and ostracism from their own people. It is almost unthinkable for the government to move against them if they do nothing more than talk.

Some intelligent, well-ensconced people, including a few who have been critical of some aspects of government policy, still insist there is no serious interference with "responsible" opposition. They will point to vociferous editorial criticisms in the English-language press, to judicial rebuffs such as the acquittal of the Treason Trial defendants, to their own moments of dissent. They seem honestly unaware of how circumspect their behavior has become, much less of how few people feel it is safe to range even as far afield as they may permit themselves to do. It is perfectly true that people whose views coincide with the government's, or who keep their views to themselves, are not likely to suffer from political repression.

But there are many others who become political eunuchs rather than invite the risks of participating, however peripherally.

The most frightened whites are often the least politically involved—people who indignantly deny they live in a police state and wouldn't be caught dead at a Liberal party meeting for fear of losing their passports.

Soon after our arrival in the Union we had an unexpected glimpse of how this kind of fear affects many who are not active in politics. Sherman often talked about an old friend with whom he had photographed wild animals on his first trip to Africa, and this friend came to epitomize the raw courage of the frontiersman at his toughest. We heard so much about his feats of derring-do that we came to refer to him as the "Brave One."

One evening Sherman visited the Brave One while Emory and I attended an interracial tea—the sort of intrepid gathering familiar to liberals and intergroup committees in states of the middle South. A genial hostess bustles around making nervous chatter while four or five self-conscious blacks, specially dressed and starched for the occasion, worry about their manners. An assortment of whites—the neurotic wife of a Protestant minister, a transient journalist alleged to be of great repute in some distant place, a timid schoolteacher proud that he has stood up for his convictions by calling a black man "mister," a bored student whose parents are active in left-wing causes—bathes the room in a beaming, shapeless goodwill. Everyone fidgets and tries to think of something to say that will be interesting but not too personal, and more or less relevant but not too controversial.

Eventually Sherman phoned to say that his friend was going to bring him by, and he wondered if they could drop in. I warned him to explain that the party was interracial before

pressing an invitation; this I heard him do, and then he reported
that his friend had said, "So what?"

They arrived a few minutes later for what must be the shortest social call on record. The Brave One took a step into the
room, saw Africans sitting here and there among the whites,
blinked, gulped, and bolted into the night without a word.

Sherman looked startled, mumbled an apology, and chased
after him. He managed to catch up about a block away, where
the Brave One angrily demanded if Sherman were trying to
"ruin" his future: "Look, man, it's all very well for you blokes
to poke about with blacks, but I've got to live here. I'd never
even get a passport so I could *get out* if I hung around a place
like that."

Sherman discovered that his description of the affair as
"interracial" had conveyed to his friend the impression that
English as well as Afrikaans-speaking guests would be present.

Of course, thousands of whites have visited in homes of nonwhites without losing their passports. But many others have lost
their passports or have suffered other consequences of official
displeasure for no apparent reason and with no possible appeal. In such an atmosphere only the most dedicated and the
most indifferent can resist the conclusion that discretion is
synonymous with common sense.

Emory and Sherman had a difficult time finding a suitable
vehicle we could afford. Notions about driving Land-Rovers
through difficult terrain died hard, but in the end they settled
for a sturdy Volkswagen that might have lasted decades on
ordinary pursuits. It never gave any trouble in towns or when
we were going to the sort of places tourists ordinarily visit.

While they were lining up a car and other provisions, I attended the annual Congress of the National Union of South

African Students, the federation of college students of the English-speaking universities, where I was to deliver a "greeting." NUSAS is open to South African students of all races, but the Afrikaans institutions have seceded rather than accept non-Europeans as equals.

NUSAS has refused to segregate its meetings, and campaigned unsuccessfully against the extension of apartheid to universities. The vigor of its adherence to nonracialism riled high government officials into denouncing NUSAS itself, and especially several of its officers, as traitors to South Africa. The customary official harassments became commonplace for people connected with NUSAS. Passports were withdrawn or denied, offices raided, mail tampered with, briefcases stolen from locked cars.

The implications of all this seemed even drearier after an addled coed was found to be tattling to the secret police about student meetings at Wits. During the ensuing uproar the Minister of Education boasted in Parliament that he maintained a network of spies in the English universities.

Then, one week before the congress was to convene, the government prevented a South West African Coloured student from leaving the country to study in Oslo on a NUSAS-awarded scholarship donated by the Norwegian Union of Students. It would have been surprising if the student, Hans Beukes by name, had been allowed to leave, for he would have been the second non-European from South West Africa *ever* to get out of the Union legally. For some reason, however, Beukes had been issued a passport only a few days before, and the only reason given for the sudden reversal was that it was in the best interests of the state. This told little, as incursions into the lives of those whom the government dislikes are always in the best interests of the state.

The peremptory treatment of Beukes seemed especially

flagrant, and stirred up an unusual storm. For one thing, an international bursary was involved. For another, Beukes had never had the remotest connection with politics, which made the repression purely and inescapably racial. And finally, the method and timing of the government's action seemed designed to intimidate the English-speaking university students on the eve of their convention: if Beukes were not to be allowed to go, the government need hardly have waited, like leopard with mouse, to pounce as he arrived to board the ship for Norway.

If intimidation had been one of the government's purposes in behaving as it did, it miscalculated badly; the chief result was an outpouring of indignation. Large groups picketed Parliament, a "Hans Beukes Fund" flourished, and many average students who had been skeptical of some of the charges NUSAS officers seemed forever to be leveling against the government found themselves convinced, and rallied behind the leadership.

This was the atmosphere as three hundred young South Africans who had been elected to represent some sixteen thousand students of all races convened in unsegregated session in the heart of South Africa's biggest city in the eleventh year of the rule of the Nationalist Government. The keynote was delivered by the Honorable Richard Feetham, Chancellor of Witwatersrand and at eighty-five one of the most revered figures in South Africa. "It is for the younger generation of whites in South Africa," he said, "realizing, as NUSAS has shown it realizes, the need for a new outlook on the whole question of the future of race relations, to persuade their elders that the time has come to face great changes, and to recognize that the only way of defending and maintaining 'Western civilization' in South Africa is not by separation and isolation, but to make a steady and generous advance toward sharing it."

The dauntless president of NUSAS, Neville Rubin, delivered the traditional Response:

"I need hardly remind you that only a month or two ago I was said to have committed high treason for informing universities abroad of the proposed legislation for university segregation. . . . In 1957 we faced the prospect of being unable to hold a congress like this through the operation of the Native Laws Amendment Act; our decision to continue to hold meetings may mean fines, imprisonment, or even lashing. . . . Only a few days ago a student who had been granted a passport to take up a scholarship offered through NUSAS was stopped when he arrived at Port Elizabeth to start his long night's journey into day. . . . Yet there is no other course open to us than to work for the abolition of ideological prejudice, despite the penalties which may follow."

The congress cheered, and got down to the tediousness of a detailed examination of hundreds of resolutions and amendments to resolutions, and to the frustrations of trying to plan strategies in open democratic session by which to carry on the grueling, unequal contest with the government. The delegates were harassed by the knowledge that spies recorded, and possibly distorted, every word they said.

Here and there voices counseled against doing anything that would further antagonize the government, at least for the moment. These must have been tempting words to many white delegates who were, after all, normal young people pursuing an education, not committed politicians, much less hardened shock troops of an underground. I wondered how long a similar group in the United States would hold out if capitulation meant all the comforts of public and official approval, and the chief visible achievement of continued resistance was a few semilegal interracial meetings.

But the greatest inducement to discouragement was an insinuating sense of isolation, of defeat as far ahead as one could see, of the futility of resistance. To many in the path of a juggernaut it is the signs of outside support that make the difference between strategy and lunacy in the decision whether to hold or flee.

These things were discussed over and over again in the jaded, sleepless intervals between sessions, and I came to feel it would be inadmissible to utter the expected platitudes for my "greetings." With government agents present, to do even that was not perhaps wise; to do anything more might imperil our getting to South West. But if I, protected by American citizenship and a ticket to Nairobi in my pocket, could be discretioned into silence, how could one expect others to speak up who had so much more to lose?

It was a risk, not calculated perhaps, but realized; but I spoke what I felt when the time came. "There may be moments," I said, "when you feel alone and isolated, but it is your tormentors, not yourselves, who are alone and isolated. Your cause is the cause of men of goodwill everywhere, and your behavior is their inspiration."

This message of support from so far away excited considerable emotion. I knew I would not again worry about the sensibilities of those who object to "outsiders meddling in the internal affairs of South Africa," when so vast a majority of her people—virtually all her nonwhites, and the bravest of her whites as well—beg and pray for such "meddling," and are indeed chiefly sustained by the hope that sooner or later it must be forthcoming in abundant measure.

III I first met Hans Beukes in Cape Town, the day after his plummet into fame. He was a depressed and disorganized young man, too shattered to plan, too frightened to fight back. He had no money and no idea where he could get any to continue his education.

I shall not soon forget how it was with Hans that day, his tall figure stooped as if something too heavy had overwhelmed his shoulders, his hands twitching, his face contorted. Behind his glasses he blinked through the tears, trying to make sense of what had happened to him. "I was always so careful," he kept saying. "I did nothing they could object to—*nothing.*"

He wanted to understand how he had offended the government, but there were no clues unless an impromptu remark made by one of the agents while ransacking his luggage be accounted one: "This bloke," the man had snorted, "has the nerve to carry commie propaganda around with him," and he waved a book by Adlai Stevenson at a colleague.

I felt sorry for Hans Beukes, but his tragedy struck me as a minor one in the sea of misery that was all around us, and his plight interested me chiefly because he was a South West African.

The Government of South Africa was to proclaim later at the United Nations that it had blocked Hans's departure because it had evidence that he planned to go to U.N. Headquarters in New York. This, as the Norwegian delegate observed, was a strange excuse to give the United Nations for taking away somebody's passport. But quite apart from that, it was a silly and dishonest afterthought. The South African Government could have had no such evidence because there was no such evidence.

The first time any thought of the United Nations entered Hans's head was when we met, *after* he had been prevented from leaving. I suggested then, not that he go to the U.N., but that he wire a protest about the seizure of his passport. At first even the idea of cabling the U.N. astounded him. He said the matter was too small compared to so many others to justify bothering a great world organization: "They wouldn't be interested in one person's education."

I explained to Hans that he had a special status as a South West African, and that he had greater significance as a symbol than as an individual; and I added that the matter would be of interest to the U.N. because whatever right the Union Government might or might not have to bar travel by its own citizens, it had no right to do such things to South West Africans. If even a Coloured of no politics were not to be allowed a passport in pursuit of higher education, what hope could there be for any other nonwhite in the Territory?

Still Hans seemed hesitant, and it was not until much later that I knew it had been a fear of presumptuousness, not a fear of the government, that had made him doubtful; so I told him that everyone would understand if he decided to preserve his neutrality and hope the government would come to approve of him at some time in the future. There I left the suggestion of the cable to the U.N., and not until a few days later did I learn that Hans had indeed sent one, and that NUSAS had sent one of its own to buttress his.

Then, toward the end of the NUSAS Congress, Hans turned up and delivered a simple little speech that electrified everyone present. He spoke without notes or artifices about his own life

and the life of his people in the district called Rehoboth in
South West Africa, and told of the events in which he had been
a central figure a week before.

Late on the night of his speech Hans caught me as I was
leaving the place of the meeting, and asked if he might talk to
me for a few minutes on a matter of great urgency. He seemed
even more nervous than he had in Cape Town the day after the
loss of his passport, and I went with him at once to a remote
spot far from the main campus. We walked in silence until
we were sure we were alone, and then he asked if I would help
him to get out of South Africa.

He said that what I had told him about the concern of the
U.N. had set him thinking; and if it was useful to cable a
protest about his difficulties, would it not be much more useful
to tell in person of the difficulties of his people? If I agreed with
this reasoning, he would try to go to the U.N. to tell this story,
but there was no one else to whom he could turn for advice
and help.

I replied that there was no doubt that a responsible person
describing the situation of the Coloured people of South West
would have great value at the U.N., but that it was a grave step
to leave without a passport, a step that would mean sacrifice
and inconvenience: a person trying to leave under such circumstances would be jailed if he were caught and stateless if
he were not.

Hans said that he knew these things but that if I felt it would
make a difference for him to talk at the U.N., he was prepared
for the consequences. I warned that no one could promise that
anything would result from his appearing at the U.N.; only he
could decide whether to take such a gamble. Then he repeated
that he had already decided to take the gamble if I were willing
to help him to get to New York. We had come full circle, so I

said we must think the whole thing out again, and we agreed
to get together in two days.

Overnight "Hans" had become a household word in South
Africa. The picketing of Parliament and the fund to provide
him with a new scholarship attracted a great deal of attention.
Opposition M.P.'s questioned the Minister of Justice, who said
that under no circumstances would the government either give
reasons for or reconsider its action: the interests of the state
required that Hans not be allowed out of South Africa, and
that was that.

The press was full of the "Beukes Affair." Numerous pictures of Hans, articles about protest rallies, editorials, and letters to the editor appeared. Overseas reactions were quoted,
and there were frequent reports on where Hans was, how he
was feeling, and what his plans were. If he happened to say he
might visit friends in Kimberley or Cape Town and then faded
from view, someone was sure to write a story announcing that
he had "disappeared," and a new rash of conjecture—"Where
Is Hans?" "Is Hans Still Here?"—would erupt.

Neither Emory nor Sherman nor I had any idea how to go
about smuggling someone out of one country and into another,
and we were not at all sure that it would be justifiable to
jeopardize again the whole project in South West. Responsible
people warned that the American Embassy would not be very
sympathetic if we were caught, and we discovered that helping
someone to leave illegally was a considerable offense under
South African law.

It was clear that the best hope of escape was through the
huge British Protectorate of Bechuanaland, which fits like a
miniature of the southern tip of Africa between the Union
and South West. Coloureds and whites do not ordinarily need

special documents to cross into Bechuanaland, but this would not help Hans if he were caught: the government would hardly allow him to do indirectly what it had just prevented his doing directly.

No one whom we could ask knew very much about security precautions or travel facilities at the Bechuanaland border, but it straggles along for a thousand miles and the crossing of it should present few problems. What worried Sherman, Emory, and me as much as getting Hans into Bechuanaland was his getting out. Once he was there he would somehow have to finish the trip to the U.N. without travel papers, and without anyone to help. There was a good deal of doubt about what the attitude of the British authorities would be, but it was not likely that they would permit someone to stay on indefinitely. Even if they did, Hans would be of no particular use to anyone bottled up in a vast semidesert.

An American visa was assured by the treaty that guarantees access to New York for people with official business at the U.N., but even with a visa and with money raised abroad we were doubtful that Hans had enough resolution or experience to get to New York on his own. The sum of our thinking was that it would make no sense to risk the undone work in South West in order to strand someone in Bechuanaland.

Hans, on the other hand, had made up his mind to go. We were astonished at how firm and vigorous he had become on the point, and the transformation affected our views: in the final analysis, his chances of getting to New York depended on how determined he was to get there. By the end of our second discussion we had promised to help in any way we could.

Those were difficult days for Hans. Whatever his offense prior to the confiscation of his passport, he had surely multiplied it afterward with his attacks on the government, not to mention the appeal to the United Nations. And his situation

was precarious in any event, for if his traveling outside South
Africa represented a threat to the state, what about his traveling inside? There was thus a certain pressure against delay, and
although we had hoped to wait until public interest in his
whereabouts had dwindled, it seemed wiser to get him out of
the country as soon as possible.

The departure from Johannesburg was a confused affair, full
of missed rendezvous and comic-opera crises.

The day began with a suggestive but fortunately vague indiscretion blurted over a tapped telephone about "Hans leaving this afternoon." Then things seemed to go well until just
after lunch, at which time Sherman was to fetch Hans in a
borrowed car and Emory was to load up the Volkswagen. They
were then to assemble, return the borrowed car, and pick me
up at the home of unsuspecting friends a few miles out of
Johannesburg. I was at the appointed place at the appointed
time, but no one else showed up; and I was abandoned to a
group of suburban matrons who carted me around to a succession of carefree tennis matches and teas, where I had to lob
and sip as if nothing else mattered.

At last I managed to get back where I had started from, and
presently Emory turned up in time to join another large group
of elegant ladies at tea. Before I could finish introducing him,
however, he was called to the phone, excused himself to
"wash his hands," and proceeded to vanish. I tried to appear
calm, but after half an hour or so the lady of the house grew
sufficiently uneasy to talk of calling the police, and we were
all enlisted in an energetic search of the estate.

Then, when the tea party had been hopelessly disrupted,
Emory reappeared as mysteriously as he had left. He seemed
surprised that anyone had noticed his absence, and explained
that he had been looking for a mailbox, which did little to

clarify matters, as it developed that a huge, brightly colored
mailbox dominated the entrance to the place.

I learned later that the call had been from Sherman, who had
asked guardedly if Emory knew where "our missing friend"
might be. Not until he had hung up did it occur to Emory that
Hans and Sherman were waiting for each other in different
places. He located Sherman and the borrowed car, but Hans
was nowhere in sight, chiefly because a number of police were
engaged in a coeducational picnic of some sort very near the
spot where he was supposed to be. Sherman then drove around
the area in the borrowed car, making as thorough a search as
he could manage while Emory waited near the place of the
missed rendezvous. Once the car passed close by Hans, who
noticed the approach of an unfamiliar vehicle and took to hiding under a bush. In this manner more time was wasted while
Hans successfully eluded Sherman, whom he thought to be the
police, until at last Sherman started to scout around on foot.

We learned a great deal from the bungling of that afternoon
about the importance of such things as precision in arrangements and the preparing of alternate plans; but it was four-
thirty before we had collected in one place and could leave for
Bechuanaland. We were several hours behind schedule, but
with luck there would still be enough time to make the border
before daybreak.

Once we got under way we moved along pleasantly enough.
Hans was full of curiosity about the northern Transvaal, which
he had never seen before, and perhaps as compensation for his
excess of caution earlier in the day, he persisted in ignoring our
warnings against peering out until a policeman noticed him
from a street corner. We could not know if the resulting
double-take was merely in reaction to an interracial carload or
if the policeman had recognized Hans. Whatever caused it, it
sent us off into a discussion of the discovery of Louis XVI en

route to the Rhenish border and helped persuade Hans to be
less conspicuous thereafter.

North from Pretoria the countryside slowly loses its color
and its towns, and west from Potgietersrust it loses its hills and
villages; and what there is of people and things in this vast
empty area is part of a redoubt of Afrikanerdom so remote and
extensive that it never fell to Englishmen even during the Boer
War.

Here a name on a map means a farm, or perhaps a store; and
"grizzled" and "old-fashioned" and "tough" are the adjectives
to tell about the isolated pioneering descendants of pioneers
who extract a living from the grudging soil. Here there are no
politics but Afrikaner Nationalist, and the black people show
no signs yet of what men must feel when they have nothing of
their own, not land or freedom nor hope of land or freedom,
and must work without cease simply to survive.

Only occasional telephone lines and motor vehicles betray
the existence of the second half of the twentieth century; and
the winds of change are as distant as the integrated classrooms
of the college in Rhodesia five hundred miles to the north, and
as unwelcome. But then suddenly even five hundred miles is not
very distant, for the second half of the twentieth century is
different from all other periods in human experience, at least
in the velocity of its winds of change.

Hours passed and we rode on into the night, trailing dust
through silent stretches of land without feature, until it was
impossible to figure out how far we were from the border. We
knew only that we ought to be there within half an hour when
all at once, with no preliminary hint of trouble, the car stopped
dead.

There seemed no reason to worry about passers-by, so we
stretched and yawned in the extraordinary glitter of the heav-

ens of the Southern Hemisphere and laughed about the afternoon's muddles, while Sherman tinkered with the motor. But
the night was cold in the manner of winter nights in the high
veld, and presently we retreated into the little car and shivered
even there. We took turns holding a flashlight for Sherman,
and offered useless advice until he suggested we would be more
helpful watching for snakes or counting the stars.

Then we fell to reviewing the various plans that had been
suggested for the entry into Bechuanaland. The border here is
the Limpopo River, and there are few bridges by which a car
can make the crossing. It would thus be easy to control and
inspect motor traffic, as the coming and going of animals had
been controlled not long before to check the spread of disease.
On the other hand, even if there were an official on duty, and
even if the official checked each passenger, the presence of a
nonwhite as baggage bearer need stir no special interest, and
there was a directness to the idea of simply driving straight
through that was appealing.

Still, after the telephone indiscretion and the startled policeman it seemed on balance a trifle reckless to leave Hans sitting
helplessly in plain view. Mr. Alfred Hutchinson, a Coloured
leader now living in exile, was to write of a similar trip to
Bechuanaland: "In trepidation I waited for the border. . . .
If the news of my escape had leaked, there I would surely be
arrested and turned back." So we talked about swimming the
Limpopo, until someone remembered a line about "the great
grey greasy Limpopo with its hungry crocodiles" (it turned
out to be more or less Kipling); and then we wondered if there
were not some better way out.

All the talk about the border helped to pass the time, but
time was passing nonetheless; and presently, from as far off as
we could see, we spotted headlights coming toward us. If it
would be unwise for Hans to be in view at the border, it would

make no better sense to risk the scrutiny and gossiping of unknown wayfarers; but the cold was biting and we wondered
if it might not be possible to hide him inside the car. The only
place in a Volkswagen that suggested itself for this sort of
thing was the area between the rear seat and the rear window.
From this neglected crevice we now removed a dilapidated
laundry bag in which we kept documents and other objects too
important to let out of reach, and in its place we poured, folded,
and twisted six feet of squirming contraband.

The proceedings were not without melodrama, what with
the headlights pressing nearer and the protesting Hans groaning and tossing in the rear. Suddenly Sherman—almost forgotten under the car—let out a whoop. The trouble, he had
discovered, was that the accelerator cable had snapped, and
with our help he thought he could fix it in a minute or two.

The headlights seemed on top of us when Sherman announced that the job was done. We rushed into the car, and
as I was piling everything loose into the cavities through which
some part of Hans might still be visible, there came the glorious
little crackle and roar that meant we were indeed under way.
Then our lights came on and stared down the hesitant ones
pulling to a stop on the other side of the road. We were in
motion now, and such are the customs of the road that two
moving vehicles, no matter how isolated from the rest of the
world, do nothing more than exchange friendly waves as they
pass in the night.

And that is how, with refinements in the distribution of
Hans's limbs and better arrangements for his breathing, we
crossed into Bechuanaland. We formulated elaborate plans to
meet contingencies none of which arose, and finally passed
peacefully over the Limpopo and out of the Union with night-
time still to spare. Then we unpiled things till Hans could be
extracted from his cache, and, like Rayne Kruger's description

of a British garrison suddenly freed from siege, startled the darkness with three cheers for the Queen.

We drove on for another hour or two, the monotony of the dust broken only by the gates that had to be opened and shut as we drove through the huge ranches which straddle the roadway. Then, near dawn, we came to a group of European-style buildings centered upon a small depot that has been given the name of Palapye Road, and in this little way station on the rail line from Cape Town to Salisbury we found a tomblike hostelry. There seemed no other place where Hans could lie low for a day or two until we had ascertained that he would not be shipped back to the Union, and until we were safely back in Johannesburg so he could turn up without confirming whatever suspicions the South African police might have had about our involvement in his departure.

It took a good deal of banging and shouting to arouse any-one at the hotel, but at last a balding man who turned out to be the manager emerged half awake and very cross. He peered at Hans through the dim light as if not sure he could trust his eyesight at such an hour, and then snarled, "You can't keep him here—get him out before I throw you all out." In the euphoria of being safely out of South Africa it had quite es-caped us that some aspects of the color bar might have pre-ceded us across the Limpopo.

I barked at Hans, as master does to servant in backward areas, and pushed him outside, leaving Sherman and Emory to register; and soon began a procession of clandestine comings and goings that were not without their awkward moments.

But for the time being all went well. We distributed our-selves along the hotel corridors and had no trouble spiriting Hans into Room 9, to which Sherman and Emory had been assigned. Then we took precautions against surprise intrusions, and slept our first sleep since we had become criminals in the eyes of a sovereign state.

When Dr. Hendrik Verwoerd cites statistics to prove that his Bantustan scheme is fair to everyone, he likes to include in his computation of the square miles he plans to give over to African use three anomalous enclaves—one of them completely surrounded by the Union—called the High Commission Territories.

None of the three—Bechuanaland, Basutoland, and Swaziland by name—is his to give, nor is it clear how he hopes to get them. All are administered by the Colonial Office in London; and Great Britain, despite speculative prophecies mumbled half a century ago in the afterglow of the Act of Union, is no more likely to hand over these areas than Kenya or Nyasaland to a despised and de-Commonwealthed South Africa. Nor, for that matter, are they any more Great Britain's to hand over; for the British have promised to consult the resident Africans before any such move is made, and have in fact already instituted a measure of self-government.

The presence of British rule so close to the Union—to say nothing of the proximity of British libertarian principles, or of the prospect of sovereign black prime ministers and parliaments on her back doorstep and within her living room—provides a daily dose of wormwood galling enough to keep the South African Government in a state of perpetual subdued indigestion. Africans, on the other hand, prize the Territories as condemned souls might cherish pockets of Purgatory shielded inexplicably from a surrounding Inferno.

The largest of the protectorates is Bechuanaland, a vast and thirsty sandpile containing as many square miles as it does people. It is innocent of industry and agriculture, and would likely have been of no interest to Europeans were it not for its geography, which makes it the corridor from the Union to the Rhodesias and thence northward through Africa. Lately have come hints of possible rich mineral deposits, but so far little has been done to develop whatever resources may lie beneath the drifting dunes. Most of the inhabitants piece out pastoral existences or go off to swell the Union's labor market.

What little is known of Bechuanaland in the world beyond is likely to have to do with the marriage of a chief of the dominant Bamangwato tribe, Seretse Khama by name, to a white girl he met while studying at Oxford. The marriage split both the tribe and the British, and the chief was exiled for a time. Now he is a member of the Cabinet of Bechuanaland and lives in Serowe with his expanding family, whose interracial presence adds to the perturbation of Afrikaner Nationalists. It was to this independent spirit that we turned for help for Hans.

Serowe, the headquarters of the Bamangwato, is a singular place, an enormous collection of native huts clustered here and there along dusty tracks that meet and fork in the European fashion. Only occasional incongruities like the concrete British administration building and a carefully measured-off playing field interrupt the absence of most of the appurtenances of the urban white man. The pleasant house of the Seretse Khamas is found easily by following the telephone line to its end. Hans was later to reside there for more than a month, the grateful beneficiary of the generosity and patience of Seretse and Ruth Khama.

But my own visit was brief. Seretse explained the regulations governing Hans's status, and we discussed his stay in Bechuanaland and the subsequent onward passage. Then we drank tea and talked of trends in history and of the responsibilities of individuals. I basked in the warmth and intelligence of this

gracious couple who had endured so much to be together, and
admired their children, handsome, friendly, and unwitting
refutations of those who see degeneracy under the bed of every
mixed marriage.

Sherman meanwhile was arranging to get word of Hans's
needs to people in London and New York. He discovered that
the telegraph official was an Afrikaner from the Union who
sneered at "black savages" and whose greatest desire was to
see Seretse Khama hang by his toes until dead: this would
teach Africans not to get ideas about white women. We abandoned the idea of phoning or cabling for help, and headed to
the hotel to write letters instead. Hans's immediate situation
was now reasonably secure, and we were eager to get back to
Johannesburg as quickly as possible so that the trip to South
West could begin without further delay.

On the outskirts of Serowe we passed the incongruous playing field. It seemed less out of character now, for there was an
excited crowd cheering an interracial soccer match. We were
the only people who appeared to notice any difference between
the white and black players. The white players were wearing
shoes, and this seemed to even things out to everyone's satisfaction.

Things at the hotel had simmered into routine. The place
was usually deserted, and we were optimistic that the periodic
ferrying of Hans to and from the washroom, and even in and
out of the hotel, had not been detected.

It was dark when we got back from Serowe. We socialized at
a desultory dinner with occasional employees and stray travelers who wandered by; conversation was invariably about the
Khamas or about an epidemic of snakebites that had taken
twenty or thirty lives. Then we retired to our rooms, Sher-

man to Room 9 with food saved for Hans, Emory and I to
pack and write the overseas letters we wanted to mail while
still outside the Union.

It was decided to leave for Johannesburg late that night in
time to cross the border in the dark. We would deposit Hans
on the road a few miles out of town, whence he should have
little difficulty in making his way to the British authorities
without any apparent connection to us.

We tried to hurry the letter writing—three copies to various
addresses in London, three others to New York—so there
would be time for a nap before starting on the long drive. But
we had not finished when the lights suddenly faded and were
gone; the local power plant shuts down at nine-thirty. So we
perched Scrooge-like over a little table and snatched whatever
quavering light we could from a feeble candle.

All at once the door to the room burst open and we found
ourselves harpooned by a giant spotlight that blinded us and
left us wriggling until I remembered that, whatever this was all
about, a man who had nothing to hide would be indignant to
have his room thus invaded. I slipped the incriminating half-
done letters into a pocket and made up in vehemence what
I had lacked in spontaneity: *What do you mean barging
into my room this way? Who are you? What do you want?*

There was no reply. The spotlight seemed to function on its
own, a piercing Cyclops independent of human direction. Behind it was the darkness, and we could see nothing. It advanced
deeper into the room, poking and probing into corners and
behind furniture. I changed from questions to orders: *Get out
of here and get that thing out of my eyes!* Then I saw Emory
slip out the door, and knew he would need time to warn
Sherman and Hans in Room 9.

Now the spotlight was retreating toward the hallway, still
playing under things and back and forth around the walls as

if a hidden panel might spring open at the last moment to reveal whatever it was looking for. Between snatches of my monologue I could hear faint sounds from down the hall, which meant Emory needed more time, so I lunged at the light and grabbed at the bulk behind it, which now emitted, of all things, sullen apologies.

"Excuse the intrusion," said a voice I had heard before but could not place.

"You'll have to do better than that," I snarled. "What are you doing bursting into someone's room in the middle of the night? I'm getting the—" But before the word came out I realized abruptly that this must *be* the manager. At least, then, it was not the authorities. Still, what if this man were to come upon a non-European illegally in his hotel, a non-European foreigner not registered, for that matter, with the appropriate officials?

It was quickly apparent that the apologies were perfunctory; the search went on. In a moment I found myself railing at empty air, and the spotlight was scouring Number 7 with the same diligence it had displayed in Number 6. Little noises still came from down the black corridor, which could only mean that all was not yet well in Number 9.

"What kind of place is this?" I was bellowing now whatever came into my head, to drown out the sounds from Number 9 and to stall the search as long as possible. "You'll get a hell of a lot of Americans to stay here when we're through telling about this!"

The door to Number 7 closed, and suddenly the spotlight was in my eyes again. "Calm down, for heaven's sake," the voice snapped. "What are you roaring about? I haven't done a blasted thing to you."

I was about to debate the point when new footsteps trailing a new light appeared from beyond Number 6—a woman in

bedroom slippers, I guessed. Before I could say very much the
pad-pad-pad of feet had ceased. "Cut all this racket!" a
woman's voice said. It was an icy, peremptory decree, and
there were distress and contempt in the words that followed:
"I'm sorry for all this inconvenience"—I realized this was addressed to me—"and you, now, stop this prowling around right
now!"

"But I tell you he's around somewhere."

"Nonsense. Always excuses. You come back where you belong."

I withdrew toward Number 9 and held my breath while the
two lights met and were pointed down, and while confused and
agitated whisperings competed, blended and competed again.
Then the man and woman followed their separate lights in the
direction that led away from Number 9, past 6, and down to the
end of the hall where a door opened. Then there was no more
light, and I knocked an all-clear on 9.

We left Palapye as we had arrived, in the crisp bleary time
when late retirers and early risers alike wish they were in bed.
Sand shone and stretched out under the headlights, and soon
we lost track of what was sand and what was sand formed
into road, and everything seemed as much a road as everything
else. We strained for signs or clues or landmarks with the tired
frenzy of mice in a maze until we chanced upon a fence and,
following it, came in time to the main route.

Then we finished the complicated arrangements with Hans
so that we could keep in touch until he was safely on his way
to New York; and put him out into the night, with warnings
about snakes and what we hoped were encouraging words of
congratulations and cheer. He was a slender, lonely figure in
the vast, inhospitable blackness, and soon he would have to
overcome the rigors of man's indifference if he survived Na-

ture's. He had come to be a friend through the vicissitudes of our few days together, a person whose intelligence and integrity we admired and whose humor and warmth we should miss. We wondered if we should ever see him again, and drove away reluctantly.

Then we proceeded without adventure until at last there appeared the gold slag heaps that meant Johannesburg in half an hour—Johannesburg where we would tell a few our route out, collect our belongings, and load and repair the car to push on quickly to South West Africa. The detour to Bechuanaland had cost four days, and we decided to leave the following noon.

But we reckoned without the Special Branch, the political arm of the South African Police.

IV We come now to the strange events of July 15th. Much of what happened I cannot explain, and it is not likely that the Special Branch will.

Early that morning I phoned some African leaders to report on the trip to Bechuanaland. The tap on the line was clumsy, and all I conveyed through the distant little clicking noises was the news that our "cargo" had been delivered safely. It was clear that the African wanted further details, and I had to say that we were planning to leave Johannesburg later in the day. I did not say where we would be going.

I decided to fly back to Johannesburg from Windhoek, to make up the time spent with Hans. That way I could stay in South West Africa several extra days while Sherman and Emory returned in the car. But when Sherman made the reservations he discovered that plane connections were such that I should need to get my visa extended by one day if any time were to be gained by flying.

I fetched the old laundry bag with the necessary documents and went to the Immigration Office, where such extensions are given in routine fashion every day. There I found myself at the end of a line of tourists that was being processed by a pleasant faded lady piled around by forms and stamping pads. She smiled mechanically as I filled out papers; then she took them to another room, as she had done with those of the people ahead of me. She did not reappear for a long time.

When she did she was very upset and said she could not extend my visa.

She was clutching a folder, and kept looking from it to me and back again, as if expecting to discover some discrepancy. I said it was ridiculous not to extend a visa for one day, and showed her my ticket to Nairobi for the day after the visa expired. She just kept saying, "I can't extend your visa; I can't extend your visa at all."

I asked if I would be put in jail if I tried to leave one day late. She seemed even more rattled than before, but all she would say was that she couldn't answer any questions. She knew only that I was not to get an extension. Then she summoned an older lady, who studied the various papers and finally announced that my only hope was the minister in Pretoria. So I left. It was about 11:15 A.M. We had hoped to start on the long drive to South West at noon.

I found Emory in the midst of last-minute errands. We agreed that my troubles at Immigration must have resulted from the phone calls and meetings with African leaders, or perhaps from the talk at the NUSAS Congress: it was too soon for the Beukes trip to have affected documents at so low a level, even if our connection with it were known.

Emory had made no speeches and had been to no meetings with Africans. He did not need to have his visa extended, but we decided to find out if the Special Branch knew of his association with me and if this association were grounds enough to blacklist him too. He went therefore to apply for an extension at the same time that I set out to track down an attorney who I hoped would call Pretoria about my situation.

Now the tale grows more complicated.

While I was at Immigration, Sherman had been in a repair shop with the car. We met as scheduled at a downtown newsstand, and I explained that our departure was to be delayed.

Sherman said it was silly to keep on lugging the old laundry bag about, but I thought I might again have need of some of the papers in it; the day seemed suddenly so uncertain.

Soon I located the attorney. I did not explain why the extra day was so important, but he agreed it was senseless for the government to insist that I be out of the country twenty-four hours before my flight was due to leave. At 11:50 A.M. he placed a call to the ministry in Pretoria and complained about the situation to an official who promised to look into it and call back by 2:30 P.M.

Meanwhile Emory arrived at Immigration, waited out the line, and filled in the forms. The lady smiled her wan smile and suggested that he apply for an extension of a month or two instead of a couple of weeks. "It can't do any harm, and you might want to stay on," she said.

Emory agreed, and the lady withdrew to get his folder. When she reappeared she was flushed and shaken, and her comments were virtually a rerun of the ones she had made to me, containing so many muttered repetitions of "I can't extend your visa" that Emory found himself wondering if she were stuttering.

At one point an elderly woman whom Emory took to be a supervisor of some sort overheard her. "But that's ridiculous," she said. She smiled apologetically at Emory and looked in the folder, then gasped and dropped it as if singed by the contact.

There seemed no way to calm the agitated women, so Emory left amid strange looks and a good deal of whispering on both sides of the counter.

Sherman spent this time arranging the car to provide as much room as possible for three passengers. He packed the four suitcases and a large box onto one side of the rear seat and into the Beukes compartment. Stray items like cameras and a radio were left on the front seat, to be squeezed later between people and under legs.

At about twelve-thirty he parked and locked the car near one of the busiest intersections in Johannesburg, and soon after that the three of us met briefly. Emory told of his adventure at Immigration. We decided to meet at two-fifteen at the lawyer's office, and then scattered to make use of the interval as best we could.

I went off to give further information to the Africans with whom I had talked on the phone, and an unsettling business it turned out to be. When we finally assembled, the Africans were sure we had been observed, and after talking for a harried five minutes while skulking in and out of dusty side streets full of cut-rate Indian stores, decaying office buildings, and second-rate teashops, we separated.

Shortly after two o'clock Sherman, Emory, and I gathered in the lawyer's office. The boys had a feeling that they had been followed, but dismissed it—too little sleep, too much nerves.

Fifteen minutes later the call came from Pretoria. A twenty-four-hour extension would be granted. Now I had to get to Immigration before the three o'clock closing time, and took off at a trot. Sherman went to get the car and was to pick me up in half an hour, at which time we would at last set out for South West.

There were no hitches at Immigration, but Sherman had not appeared by closing time so I headed for the corner where the car had been parked. En route I bumped into Emory, who had been running to fetch me and who looked more disconcerted than I had ever seen him look before. He gasped out the news that the car had been broken into and all our luggage stolen.

Someone had shattered the glass in the vent window by the

driver's seat, but it was indeed a peculiar theft, for the cameras and other lucrative items that had been loose in front were still there. Only the suitcases and the box that Sherman had stacked in the back had been taken. These contained all our clothes except those we were wearing.

The question of what else the suitcases contained was more troubling, but we realized at once how fortunate we had been that the things we needed most had not been in the car at all: passports, travelers' checks, and the documents about South West were safe in the laundry bag. We could recall no potentially awkward items that had been in the suitcases except a few carbon copies of letters asking for financial assistance.

Not that the full implications of the theft occurred to us right away. We filled out reports at the police station and bought some clothes in a dilapidated shop whose proprietor clucked sympathetically about the outrageous crimes perpetrated by Africans in Johannesburg. Our financial distress so stirred him that he even lowered his prices. For that matter everyone wanted to help atone for this misadventure that might mar the impression of South Africa that we would take home with us. The police were especially sympathetic, and we heard over and over again about the dreadful problem presented by the presence of so many criminal Africans who had no respect for property.

But with second wind the idea that the theft had been the work of Africans began to seem less plausible. Several minutes would be required to break into a locked car and make off with four large suitcases and a box; it was not easy to picture nonwhites undertaking such a venture at the height of the midday rush in the presence of hundreds of passers-by. Furthermore, ordinary thieves would be unlikely to ignore five fancy cameras and the other equipment that lay at the fingertips of whoever had broken in.

The theft had occurred while we were all gathered in the lawyer's office. This was the only time that more than a few minutes had passed without any of us wandering by the car, and only someone watching us could have known that during this interval we would be safely out of the way. And there was a suspicious sequence to the events of the day. At 11:00 A.M. I am refused a visa extension; at 11:50 a strong protest is lodged at the Ministry of External Affairs. Would it be unreasonable to guess that the Special Branch might then have been asked to justify an arbitrary and apparently stupid ruling and that, lacking evidence with which to do so, it set out to procure whatever documents might be available in our luggage? At 2:10 P.M. we are out of range to await word from Pretoria, and at 2:20 the luggage is stolen.

When my comment on the tapped phone that we would be leaving Johannesburg that day is added to the other circumstances, the timing as well as the unusual nature of the theft seemed suggestive. Thus we were not very surprised when three months later the South African Government attempted to buttress its attack on us at the U.N. with quotations from one of the carbons that had been in the luggage.

In retrospect, I think that night was the most critical of the whole journey. Without companions of such spirit and determination, I might have been overwhelmed by the logic of a good night's rest and a search for the stolen clothes the morning after. And had there been further delays then, there would be very little more to write about now.

At best we would have traded a few hours of fretting in bed for a crucial day in South West—a day, as things turned out, that would have made the difference between missing and making contact up and down the line. Spirits were drooping, but further postponements could hardly help: it was one thing to fail trying, quite another to fail to try. Cumulative delays had planted a gloomy suspicion that we might never get around to undertaking what we had, after all, come so far to do. To remain in Johannesburg any longer, like sitting ducks too scared or too stupid even to make the chase interesting, seemed demented. It was Sherman who blurted what we were all thinking: "Let's get on with it," he said, "before we fold up."

We had no way of knowing what the Special Branch was up to, which may have made it seem more nearly omniscient than it was. Did it suspect yet that Hans was out of the country, and if so did it know how he had got out? How much more suspicion would it take to deport us than to refuse to extend a visa for twenty-four hours? We wondered too if the carbons would give away enough of our plans to cause us to be headed off before we got to South West.

And so, exhausted, luggageless, and somewhat unnerved, we set out at midnight on the long drive. Even when we had the road to ourselves in open country, the imagination conjured up roadblocks in each new distant town, roadblocks in sleepy *dorps* where mystified local constables would search the passing car or bark incoherent questions at us in resentful 3:00 A.M. Afrikaans. Each road sign announcing an impending community caused a new flurry of plans to outwit nonexistent new obstacles. But gradually the signs became fewer, the fears seemed sillier, and fatigue deepened until it overtook us; and we took turns sleeping as the veld petered out into wilderness and then choked in the sand of great arid wastes.

Sherman's diary tells the story of our arrival in South West: "Desolate drive—thick dust—we are covered, almost buried, coughing and blowing—we go into drifts. Few signs of life."

And this indeed was South West. Dust, dust, and more dust —dust in your mouth if you tried to talk, in your eyes when you looked up, in the gears of the car, in sandwiches or thermos bottles tucked far under everything, into scalps beneath protecting caps.

By the second night we had made it through the natural barriers, and faced the newer man-made ones. We were at the sort of outpost we had discussed so often in abstractions; and now somehow we had to find the right African—the one who presumably knew some white men were coming who were friends, who were to be trusted and hidden and taken to the people in their homes and then passed along to helping hands at the next place.

Several times we were to repeat the strange rite: the leaving of the car to search on foot for the proper shack or kraal, the groping for contact with frightened, suspicious Africans, the frustration of unknown languages, the tension of understanding nothing of the whispered conference about yourself, the trek through the dark to another shack or kraal, the discovery of an African who spoke a little English or broken German, the offering of a handshake and the mumbling of vague pleasantries that you hope will establish that you are not a white man like the other white men who have come this way; and then the waiting out of the indecision: Who is this baas who offers his hand and greets us with words of friendship? And why does he come to us in the dark and ask to see the one among us who is most active against the other baases?

Soon we were more knowledgeable in the local ways, and the task was simpler. Then word of the presence of "friends from America" spread so far among Africans that passwords and suspicious conferences were replaced, sometimes carelessly, by triumphant receptions and welcoming parties. And then we faced a different kind of problem, the problem of leaving some hope without leaving too much hope. For Jane Kerina had been right. The years of isolation had left a great

yearning for encouragement, for any sign of help from outside; and often we found ourselves regarded as the forerunners
of more substantial help, the first response to years of petitions
to the United Nations or even of years of prayers to the Al-
mighty.

But I came close to failing the night of the first effort to
establish liaison.

Emory and Sherman had dropped me at the edge of a town,
and soon I was on my first foray into a South West African
Location. There was something quiet and removed about the
place—this was not one of Johannesburg's mammoth slums,
not Alexandra or Moroka swallowing the stranger in its vast
throbbing belly. Half the Location seemed to glance or stare
at me as I passed hovels and stirred up dust and wondered how
to find the building where I was to ask for my contact. The
Africans who saw me steered clear or bowed, and I knew they
were sure my presence boded no good; and I felt the shame of
being white where white men have so comported themselves
that terror is their trademark to nonwhites.

I had walked along thus in the ambiguity of my plans for
perhaps ten minutes when I saw not far away the fence that
I knew I must avoid, for there would be the guards controlling
the comings and goings from the Location. I cut sharply to the
left, and in a few minutes found myself in the doorway of a
collapsing little hut in whose squalid center an ancient woman
was poking at something liquid in a great pot. Seven or eight
ragged souls lurked here and there around her, apparently oblivious to an eerie smoke that floated up from a brazier beneath
the pot.

I was as startled as the Africans, and tried to apologize for
intruding; but no one understood anything. Then I tried in
halting syllables to find out how to get where I wanted to go,
but this was useless too. So I withdrew, bowing out backward

like a courtier before an Oriental potentate, grinning as broadly as I could and uttering soothing noises; all of which must have puzzled the people in the hut and done little to assuage their fears. When I was outside again and safely unbent I looked back to find two pairs of frightened eyes glued to me through an empty place that served as window for the near wall of the hut.

I thought: *It's not the laws or even the poverty that are the worst thing; the worst thing is the terror.* The worst thing is to exist at the whim of a race of people each of whom represents danger; so that soon the eyes are always clouded, the stomach always tense, the emotion always fear. *It would be bad enough to be always at the mercy of someone else even if the someone else had mercy.*

Later I went again to this first living place I had visited in South West Africa, and learned that nine people did indeed stay there and that such crowding is not unusual in the Location. Whatever may be said in extenuation of slums in the Union—the vast influx of Africans to urban areas is the general explanation—hardly applies in such places as this one. Any government concerned about the living conditions of its people could provide decent housing for the relatively small numbers involved here; it is quite impossible for Africans to provide decent housing for themselves on a wage that averages less than $7 per month.

I continued to cross the Location and at length spotted an African wearing a jacket and tie. He responded in German when I asked directions, and led me to the building I was looking for. There my arrival caused a good deal of confusion, in addition to the customary scurrying and groveling. Clearly no one had been expecting me, or any other white man, and no one was about to admit to any knowledge of the people I was supposed to find. It is remarkable how determination not to cooperate can be preserved through layers of the most obsequious deference.

It occurred to me that dealing with several people at once was bound to multiply mistrust. If, for instance, one of the Africans present were not considered reliable by the rest, there could hardly be candid replies to my questions. Furthermore, it was hardly sensible to entrust my own security to more mouths than absolutely necessary.

So I started to leave, and thanked everyone for their kindness. There was one waspish little man with whom I thought I had sensed some hint of rapport through all the barriers; perhaps it was just that his English was so much the best of any of the Africans present. I turned to him as I walked out into the dust: "Would you be so good as to show me the shortest route to town?" There was no easy way to decline such a request, and he joined me as the others went back into the building.

"Now take me somewhere where we can talk alone for a few minutes," I said, and soon we were in a little room notable for a floor and ceiling that were not the earth and the sky.

I suppose I had hoped privacy would work a miracle, but it did not. I tried to sound more confidential when I repeated my request for information, but all I could elicit was the comment that he had already told me all he knew. His eyes narrowed, whether from suspicion or hardness hardly mattered. I was still the enemy, and that was that.

For my part I wondered how far I dared go in revealing credentials to a stranger. His hostility made me want to trust him, and I went partway with an explanation of my inquiries that included a vehement denunciation of apartheid but skirted the specifics of what I was after.

"Many men denounce things they serve," the little man remarked, but I thought the earnestness of my tirade had made a dent; and then he went to the heart of the matter: "Why, sir, do you wish to see these men so urgently?"

Why indeed! "I have come a long distance to give them a message, and to ask certain questions that could be helpful in their work."

"What message, sir? What questions? Helpful in what work, sir?"

And so we fenced, inching closer to trust. I became more and more convinced that such evasion was too unyielding to be a pose; and I thought he sensed something genuine in the manner of my persistence. I played with the idea of producing one of the letters from Kerina, but this step still seemed too final: words once said could not be unsaid, but they could be denied; documents once displayed could be searched for, and then must be destroyed or left to endanger everything.

I tried a new tack instead. Perhaps, I said, he could answer these questions himself. And perhaps then I could give him a message to pass along to the people for whom I was looking.

Now curiosity flickered across his face, and I put inquiries about life in the Location. Now it was he who was on the spot, for if such questions can be noncommittal, the way they are answered must tell much. While he hesitated, I had a belated hunch and added another question, concerning the condition of a well-known African of the area whose illness had lingered on until it had become a matter of great concern. "If there is no treatment for him here, I have money to send him to a place where such sickness may be helped."

"You know of this man and wish to help him?"

I thought: *That* document I can show you, for it cannot compromise one too seriously to greet an invalid and offer financial assistance; and I took from my pocket a letter that had come with instructions about this sickness. He looked at the letter and then up at me, and for the first time our eyes met.

"The ones you seek are no longer here. One has been banned, and we do not know where the government has put him. The other has had to go back to the Reserve. We are all in special danger now. When they use the ban once, it is usually soon used again on those who replace the one who is banned. You must understand our caution—it is not excessive with such things going on. Perhaps I can help you, since the others cannot, but we must move on from this place. I shall fetch some of our people, and you may put these questions to them if you wish. Can we meet again in an hour?"

So the first contact was made, and we were on our way across this vast territory, dodging from tribal Reserve to shantytown, and then on to the next Reserve, talking always with Africans, taping their stories on our machine, examining and photographing their living conditions. Most of the time we traveled together in the Volkswagen; the stealing of the baggage made the car seem almost roomy, and each of us learned to sleep in the foetal postures permitted by the back seat.

Whenever possible we met with Africans after dark, when detection was more difficult and less likely: fewer police are on duty at night, and fewer Europeans are on the move. A number of times the car broke down while we were ferrying an African illegally, and white passers-by insisted on stopping to help. Usually we succeeded in waving them on with grateful smiles, but one very cold night a truck stopped and its driver would not be dissuaded. He was a gruff, friendly Afrikaner who was sure our protests meant merely that we were reluctant to bother him with our difficulties. The cab of the truck was empty except for the driver, but in the open part behind the cab, as is the custom of the place, there was an old African who was shivering so violently that we wondered how he held together when the truck was moving.

Our passenger was too well known in the area to risk being seen, and was flat on the rear seat, bundled so that he looked like old clothes strewn carelessly over a sack of something shapeless. Sherman and the driver had started tinkering around in the rear of the Volkswagen when all at once we heard the Afrikaner explain that he knew exactly what the trouble was: it was the battery—which in a Volkswagen is located beneath the rear seat! Sherman managed to insist long enough that he had just checked the battery for the passenger to slip out of the car and into the surrounding darkness.

There were occasions when we separated, to save time or to minimize conspicuousness, but with only one car three-way divisions were a headache. Communication and transport being what they were, the law of averages treated us well if two reappeared on time. There was no rule about how to proceed if someone were missing, and no way to prevent the imagination from conjuring up all sorts of mishaps that might have befallen the absent partner.

During the early part of the trip we tried to avoid spending time in areas where our presence might come to the attention of journalists or officials, but it was far more important to avoid being noticed conferring with Africans or visiting illegally in African areas. The police must have realized soon after our arrival in South West that something out of the ordinary was going on in certain African areas, but there was nothing to connect us with these goings-on, and whatever vague suspicions they might have had represented no immediate threat to us.

There were, however, occasional liaisons that had to be made in daylight in the European parts of towns. Africans were terribly nervous about meeting us where the rendezvous might be noticed, and while we did not fully share these fears we did of course understand them.

I recall a number of such liaisons which followed similar patterns. I would get out of the car in the fringe section of a European area and walk past an appointed spot at an appointed moment, glancing at any Africans in view. As a rule I had only the vaguest idea of what the man I was to meet looked like; hopefully some identifying characteristic would point him out. I would examine objects in windows or on the street until I spotted a likely African; then would follow a good deal of circling around, accompanied by a careful scrutiny of all Europeans in the area. If any seemed unduly interested in either of us we would avoid crossing paths, and on one such occasion the African vanished for so protracted a period that I wrongly concluded he was not the man I was looking for.

When the tentative probings had evolved into confidence that we were indeed who we were supposed to be, and when the coast seemed clear of possible snoopers, we would manage to exchange a greeting without stopping to talk to each other. Ordinarily this would consist of a series of monosyllables mumbled as we passed, going slowly in opposite directions:

"Three o'clock."

"Today?"

"Second light, bottom of hill."

"In the car."

"Right. Till then."

Theoretically I was to produce one of the letters of introduction, but I think most of the Africans would have preferred singing a stanza of "God Save the Queen" to scrutinizing a document while I stood by on a city street. In fact the key to establishing contact was invariably the eyes—some look blended of expectancy, inquiry, hesitation and recognition communicated itself long before anything was said.

Sometimes there was a long journey between the place of rendezvous and the place where discussions and an inspection of conditions were to occur. We saw a good deal of the hinterland on excursions such as these, and tasted something of the daily lives of non-Europeans, something of the weary quicksand struggle to fend off starvation and to avoid being beaten or jailed for another day.

We came to feel we understood the vast, brooding despair that sits silently everywhere when ten thousand inevitable tomorrows loom worse than ten thousand grim yesterdays, when there is never a hope of getting ahead of today so that tomorrow can be better, or even so that the tomorrow of the children can be better. Sometimes we imagined that we understood the physical toll of living always with disease, of subsisting on a diet whose mainstay is a tasteless porridge called mealie meal which may be served up in a variety of guises but which does not vary in the inadequacy of its food value.

But how do you understand such a despair when you have experienced none of the yesterdays and will presently escape even the anticipation of the tomorrows? And how do you understand such a physical toll when you are made of a lifetime of all the milk and meat and fruit you can consume, and when even now if you nibble of the mealie meal you are free to supplement it later; or even to avoid it entirely in the logic of not risking stomach troubles that might impede the progress of the trip?

Indeed Emory and I found it wise to be careful about what we ate, but Sherman has a digestive apparatus that is gargantuan, and impervious to ordinary upsets. Occasionally we were confronted by the familiar choice of downing some noxious-looking local delicacy or offending people whose friendship we hoped to have, but these moments never posed a problem if Sherman's stomach were nearby. If it was sometimes irksome never to be done feeding it, its broad tastes made it a simple thing to keep stoking even in the most woebegone places.

It was also handy to have Sherman around when drinking became a problem, because neither Emory nor I drinks. We found ourselves in a number of situations where to refuse some alcoholic offering would have invited resentment. Fortunately we could all accept drinks when they were proffered, and then quietly switch our glasses or their contents to Sherman, which gratified him and spared us.

We became such artists at plying Sherman secretly with liquor designed for us that one night at an isolated mission things almost got out of hand. Sherman obviously savored whatever it was that a jolly missionary was pouring into our cups, so we kept on uttering grateful phrases and relaying our share on to him. This was all very well for the first three rounds or so, by which time even Sherman's capacity began to be taxed. But by then there was no convincing our hosts that our thirst was quenched, and Sherman somehow made it through two or three more rounds. At that point he was relaxed enough to launch into a report of a complicated dream he claimed to have had about flotillas of death-dealing birds that turned out to have human faces. When the harpies began to acquire the facial characteristics of members of the South African cabinet, I grew alarmed and began singing to drown out further discussion.

This sent Sherman off into a series of offkey duets with an Eydie Gormé record, accompanied by a number of clerics who beat time with the zeal of a tribal drum corps trying to get an urgent message through to the next village. Even so it was better than having to contend with the predatory swooping of the death-dealing harpies.

Wherever we went the story for the black man was the same: terror, poverty, isolation, oppression. I came to understand the words of Kozonguizi that had so puzzled me long before. For here, unlike the Union, there are no resident foreign correspondents and few travelers to focus world attention. There are virtually no sympathetic Europeans, and there is not a single African doctor, lawyer, engineer, or college graduate of any kind to buffer the simplicities of unchallenged white domination.

Even the pass laws are more oppressive than in the Union. An African who wishes to leave his Location to visit in a Reserve or in another Location must first get separate permits from the white officials where he lives and from those where he wishes to go. Moreover, tribes are to be segregated one from another *within* Locations, and it is proposed that special permission be required to visit a person of another tribe who lives in the same Location.

I met one young man whose mother had become ill in an African area some forty miles from his own. Three days were required to collect the necessary permits, and when at last the young man arrived at his mother's place he found her dead. He would have chanced the trip without official sanction had he realized how sick she was, but what must it do to a man to miss a last visit with his mother because of such a law?

Everywhere we were told that we were the first whites, other than occasional missionaries, with whom Africans had been able to meet as equals, let alone as friends, in many years— sometimes the first ever. There were differences in customs and attitudes between rural and urban Africans, and between members of this tribe and that. But there was also a common denominator that undermined everything else: the common denominator of unvarying mute misery—a misery compounded of poverty and fear until there seemed no way to filter out the one from the other. If you are black you are poor, and if you are black you can do nothing to change either your blackness or your being poor. So having nothing and doing nothing fuse like chewing and swallowing, and only the occasional exception reminds you that these are separable functions.

You are ill, too ill to work, and you stay home after years without a day missed. The police raid house to house in the Location and find you in your bed. You explain that you are ill, and are beaten until the police grow tired of the sport. Then you are arrested, for no one is allowed to stay away from work without first securing the permission of the white employer. But if you are particularly useful to the white employer, or if he is a kind man and you have not before been absent for many months, he may fetch you from the prison and pay your fine, subtracting it from your wages; and you will bow the head and smile and say, "Thank you, Baas." You scrimp four months to buy a ticket for the train to visit the family of your wife ninety miles away. You get the necessary permits, buy the necessary ticket, and then the white man will not let you on the train. There are no reasons given, but you bow the head and smile and say, "Thank you, Baas."

The stomachs and spirits of those who endure such permanent tactical quiescence pay a frightful price for repressing so much that is natural. But the price of behaving otherwise is incalculably worse. Hans Beukes told of this state of affairs at the U.N. His testimony bore mainly on the situation as it confronts Coloureds, whose treatment is in fact considerably less brutal than that of Africans:

"Assaults take place as often as there is a nonwhite person who dares to assert his self-respect and show what they call cheekiness and insolence. While teaching in Karasburg in 1957 I was manhandled and vilely abused in one of the banks by one of the clerks for having reported his offensive and insulting treatment of me at an earlier occasion to the manager.

"Our people have frequent occasions to be inflamed by the brutalities their kin have to suffer, but they have to remain silent, because there is no point in going to the courts. Cases come not infrequently of employers ill-treating their employees, but in practice assault and ill-treatment are more common than indicated by the number of cases reaching any court. Many people suffer in silence because, firstly, they are ignorant of their rights before the law; and secondly, the experience of so many others before the courts in cases between black and white make them skeptical of ever obtaining justice. They might, instead of getting justice, fare worse and even be assaulted by the police for attempting to challenge the authority of the 'baas' before the case reaches the court. . . .

"The fines for breaches of the pass and other minor laws are severe. In Windhoek, last year, I saw the three-minute trial of a tribesman from the north who came there to search for work. He was fined £10 or forty days for lacking the proper permits; £10 would be the wages of about three to five months for him.

"It is no longer possible for one to travel through the Territory unmolested by the police and others. In February last year, going home from Swakopmund, a coastal town, by rail, I was hauled off the train at Windhoek along with two other men by two private clothes policemen. They traveled up and down the train summarily searching the person and luggage of every nonwhite person. I had fifteen .22 cartridges in my possession, and the two gentlemen, both of them elderly and respectable, had failed to comply with some statute or other. One of them was en route to Port Elizabeth in the Union, and had to interrupt his journey in Windhoek for three days as a

result of the arrest. The policemen demanded passes from all
the black passengers, and I saw one of them slap and kick a
passenger who had dared to question the authority of an
ordinary white man, as he thought the policeman was, to
interrogate him."

Even people suspected of no infringement of any regulation
are not free from the attentions of the police, who reach everywhere and terrify all nonwhites; which is, after all, one of their
functions.

One morning, while wandering through the part of Windhoek where the European business area frays off into African
slums, I noticed on a side street a stately Herero lady playing
with a dog. She was dressed in the elegant robes and headdress
of the Herero women that so mock European efforts to picture
the African as a hopeless sloven. Balanced impossibly on her
head were a pail and some packages. The dog was barking
and wagging its tail; the lady was petting it; and visible in the
background were the shacks and dust that mark the beginning
of the African Location.

I hurried toward the lady, smiled, pointed to my camera,
and asked if she would mind petting the dog a moment longer
while I took a picture. There was some difficulty communicat-
ing precisely what it was I wanted, for white men do not often
approach African women on the streets of Windhoek with
such purposes in mind, but at last everything was set. Even
the dog seemed to be cooperating. Then suddenly, out of
nowhere, descended an Afrikaner policeman who had apparently been gazing at our little scenario for some time.

I wondered what we had done that had offended any tentacle
of apartheid, and worried about petitions to the U.N. and
exposed film that were on my person, but at first the policeman
hardly seemed to notice me. He battered the woman with a
torrent of noisy Afrikaans. She clutched the dog and looked

around terrified, first toward the haven of the Location and then at me.

A few minutes of this crumbled my resolve to say nothing; the least I could do was to offer an apologetic explanation. This I did, to the general effect that the whole affair was my fault, not the lady's, and that I was terribly sorry if we had committed some sort of offense.

The only effect of this intervention was to confirm whatever suspicions the policeman may already have had that I was a foreigner, and to turn his attention to me. "That's the trouble with you people," he growled in guttural English. (It wasn't clear to me *what* people.) "Always pampering the natives."

He seemed uncertain how to proceed. Perhaps he was wondering if this were sufficient explanation to a foreigner for his treatment of the woman. "And her mistreating that little animal. They have no human feelings, none at all," he said, meaning the woman. Then, waving his club in her direction and barking in English, he ordered her to turn the dog loose, which she did.

The dog stayed where he was, licking her shoes, and we stood around in awkward silence. The only thing that came into my head was some lines from *The Gondoliers:*

> *Your polite attention touches*
> *Heart of Duke and heart of Duchess*
> *Who resign their pet*
> *With profound regret,*

so I remained speechless, ashamed of my caution and afraid I might not be able to sustain it. But I shall not soon forget the terror and hate in the eyes of the African woman as she stood upright and dignified, still balancing her pail and her packages, a civilized human being at the mercy of a barbarian, while a cipher stood silently by and thought of lines from Gilbert and Sullivan.

The incident really ended there, insofar as it ended anywhere. The dog released, the policeman moved toward me, but just as I started to fear the worst he said in confidential, almost paternal tones that I must beware of the criminal Kaffirs—the club began to wave toward the woman again—who otherwise would steal the clothes off my back and ruin my holiday. I tried to smile (this seemed to confirm that I was indeed a stranger on holiday), mumbled something polite, apologized to the lady for having delayed her, and left as calmly as I could. The club was still waving and the policeman was again shouting as I passed beyond earshot.

I relived the whole affair many times afterward—the shame at my cowardice, the concern about the ultimate fate of my partner in crime and a fleeting satisfaction that I had at least managed to communicate an apology to her in leaving, the curiosity about whether I would have behaved better if I had not been laden with incriminating matter; above all, the sickness of humiliation and impotence lingering in the stomach.

These are not things to forget, not even if you are white and hence not a direct victim of such things personally, not even when the perpetrators of such things spread hospitality and kindness around you like some pleasant-smelling salve applied to the wrong wounds.

V The home of Hans Beukes in South West Africa is in an enclave called Rehoboth which, like its biblical namesake, is a peaceful and roomy spot on the fringe of a desert. We paused there to bring news of Hans to this place that is now the scene of some of the strangest workings of the white man's strange laws.

Rehoboth is neither Reserve nor town, even as the great majority of its inhabitants are neither black nor white. Here is clustered the Coloured community of the Territory, backed off the main rail and auto route through South West like a hump on a spine. Because the people are not white, they are poor, and have no voice in the general government of the Territory. But because they are not black they are free to come and go without passes, and for many years enjoyed a political autonomy guaranteed by treaty.

Whatever the uncertainties of so in-between an existence in the rest of the Territory, in this little duchy the Coloured man has status and is not stuffed into the wrong end of a white man's city. Coloured farmers own their own land, and Coloured tradesmen cater to Coloured customers. Coloured burghers elect their own *raad* (council) to administer their own affairs. When the "sacred trust" of the Mandate replaced imperial German rule, there was even hope for a time that the distant government of the white man would now come in friendship so the children of Rehoboth might be taught in better schools and the people might learn better ways to use the soil; and that with such help there might come a dent in poverty and an easing of the harshness of life.

The land in Rehoboth is richer than much of the land that lies around it, and many of the people work on farms. But there is a picturesque little central district built out from churches, where a man passing through could almost imagine that he had stumbled into a village in southern Castile. Expressionless people dressed in the shapeless clothes of peasants amble through dusty streets under a hot sun, past ancient houses kept tidy on the outside despite the absence of barest necessities within.

The arrangement is of course a segregated one, with all the ramifications of such arrangements; but it is not one bullied into existence or artificially extended. There has been a gradual weakening of the traditional disdain for Africans, although they still live in a separated area; and there have long been farms in Rehoboth rented by Europeans. Indeed, the economy of Rehoboth depends on her agriculture, and many Coloured landowners, especially during the current drought, have in turn depended on cash paid in by their wealthy white tenants.

But when the government of the white man came at last, it was discovered that such a situation is a threat to racial purity; and soon the people began to feel that the government had come not to teach and to heal, but because the white people were covetous of the land that for so many decades had belonged to the Coloureds. For now it is said that white farmers may not rent land from nonwhite owners, and the white tenants must leave, no matter their own preferences or the consequences to Rehoboth. The reason given is the impartial fairness of the white man's law, but it will be observed that the effect of such a law is to drive the Coloured man to sell his farm to the white and to live where he must turn his labor to the white man's needs. And to enact such laws the authority of the raad must be humbled, no matter the pledges and treaties thus dishonored, for it would never agree to legislate in this manner.

Hans spoke of this at the U.N.:

"When the Union assumed the Mandate, it forced our people to accept its laws in contravention of its own agreement with them. My grandfather and eight other leaders escaped death by a firing squad for alleged rebellious activities, through the intervention of the League authorities, for their opposition to this.

"White tenant farmers in our area have recently been ordered to leave on the termination of their leases. . . . Many of our people who do not have the capital to develop their farms or stock them, and who are dependent on the white tenant farmers, will be left without a source of income.

"How hard our people try to make a decent living, in spite of enforced difficulties, but it soon becomes apparent how their attempts are bogged down by the odds against them. Poverty and ignorance are the determinants of the way of life of most of our people. There is no instruction by government agencies of the nonwhite farmers, and no assistance for development or instruction in scientific methods of farming is made available to them. All this is made available to European immigrants with good results.

"Many people are at present unemployed. The majority of these people who have no income from farming have to find other means of subsistence. The opportunities for gainful employment are very limited in the Rehoboth area. For that reason many people have to emigrate temporarily. Of the total population—about 18,000—more than half are out of the area at any one time, working on farms and in the towns.

"Wages are seldom more than £5 per month; they range more commonly between £2 and £4. All farm workers and

most others are at the absolute mercies of their employers
backed by the law. There are no minimum wage rates established by the law. There are no trade or labour unions or
their distant likelihood.

"Then the pitiful figure these people must naturally present
—underfed, underclad, and generally demoralized—is more
often than not used as proof of their human inferiority, and
then again as justification that they do not need as much as
the white man does."

There exists a people whose experience with the ways of
apartheid has been even stranger than that of the people of
Rehoboth. These are the Nama people, and they have been
adjudged Africans in South West but Coloureds in the Union.

In South West they are to be "developed," in the sensitive
phrasing of the law, along the tribal lines prescribed by the
Bantu Education and Bantu Authorities Acts, and the teaching of their children is to be governed by the Minister of Native
Affairs' notions of what Africans are fit to learn. But cross the
Orange River and they must not be developed in these patterns
at all; indeed, to use the same syllabus to teach the same child
would be to commit a crime against the state.

It is easy to understand the confusion of the South African
Government about the racial status of the Namas. They are
brown-skinned, not black, and there is a slant to the eyes that
with their high cheekbones and narrow noses suggests Oriental
rather than African origin. Still, they do not enjoy the wonders
of white blood, and neither in his theology nor in his legal arrangements has the Afrikaner Nationalist a proper place for
a man who looks like a mulatto but is not one.

The Nama chiefs have spurned the financial enticements of
the Bantu Authorities Act and rejected its cession of traditional tribal freedoms. As punishment they have been stripped

of power and forbidden to travel more than a few miles in any direction without special permission.

The greatest of these chiefs, Hendrik Samuel Witbooi, is a vigorous, articulate man in his fifties, with the hands and shoulders of a dirt farmer and the bearing of an exiled noble. When he spoke to us he was vehement in his contempt for the "lie" of self-government promised in the Bantu Authorities Act, and indignant about the Bantu Education Act:

"The government tells me that if I accept their Bantu Authority Act I will be given more authority, but I realize that by giving me this Act the government is destroying even the little rights which my people have had so far.

"All the Nama headmen told the administration we totally do not want the Bantu Authority Act. They want puppets to do their work. But we are not puppets; we are chiefs. We also do not accept that Nama tribal fund which is related to the Bantu Act. We have said, 'It must be buried. Let it never again sound in our ears.' Although this government says that he is not forcing us to accept anything, yet we see that this government is forcing us, or the government would have weighed what we have to say. . . .

"In this country we do not want different systems of education for children of different races. If they wish to make an Education Act, let it be an Education Act to put the key in the lock and unlock the door. That is all that our children need. But now the teachers who have to teach other children were just taught only as far as Standard Two [fourth grade]. How can a teacher who has only got Standard Two teach other children?"

His appeal to the U.N. concluded as follows:

"The Union Government has ruled South West Africa for thirty-nine years as a Mandatory, and if I include all that this government has done for us in that thirty-nine years then I have found nothing. We have no opportunity, no education; we have no political rights. You have no rights in the house in which you are sleeping. . . . Instead of becoming better, our life situation becomes more and more worse.

"We, the indigenous inhabitants of this country, have totally no sort of freedom; we have no freedom of thought, we have no freedom of speech, we have no freedom of religious worship. All in which we are kept is fear. This is why we have approached the United Nations Organization after we hear that it is such a great organization."

Chief Witbooi also talked at some length about the situation that had arisen in a Reserve called Hoachanas, which is occupied by the Rooie Nasie tribe, whom the chief described as the "first Nama people ever residing in South West Africa."

No sharper dispute over fact has arisen between appeals received at the U.N. from Africans and pronouncements of the Union Government, than the controversy over Hoachanas. It has centered upon two questions—the quality of the land at Hoachanas and at a place called Itzawisis, and the wishes of the Rooie Nasie people. The whole matter was high on the list of items we hoped to explore at firsthand.

The administration has ordered the Rooie Nasie tribe, which has lived in Hoachanas since before 1700, to move to a new location 150 miles away at Itzawisis. It has explained that this order is motivated by a desire to increase the amount of land available to the tribe and that the move to Itzawisis is for the benefit of the Africans themselves, who would in fact welcome it were it not for the machinations of a few agitators. The petitions sent to the U.N. have insisted that the land at Itzawisis is uninhabitable and that the people will never agree to go.

The most important figure in the controversy was the minister of the African Methodist Episcopal Church at Hoachanas, a man named Markus Kooper, whose leadership is constantly praised in the Rooie Nasie appeals and was tacitly confirmed when the administration forcibly deported him to Itzawisis in advance of the tribe. We decided to talk with him as soon as we found an African who could take us to him. At last we met a man in a town not far from Itzawisis who said he would do so, and the next morning we set out on the last lap to Itzawisis and Markus Kooper.

Soon we left the main road and made our way on narrow tracks between which the earth rose in mounds that seemed designed to fit between the wheels. Occasionally we came to what had once been a river, and there were times when the best place to drive was in the bed of some stream dry now through four years of drought. Then the scraping and scratching sounds from under the car stopped, and it was easy to forget what misery this perverted waterway meant to those who had better uses for it than to drive along its parched floor. Sometimes the trail seemed to peter out entirely, and we wondered if even the unruffled guide might not have become confused in the vast tan sea that piled and drifted from horizon to horizon and snickered at the picayune creatures coughing and spitting along her endless bottom.

At last we came upon a great fence whose presence interrupted the wasted emptiness of nature to announce that man had staked his claims even here where there seemed nothing to claim. On the fence were two signs, back to back, one reading "Wasser" and the other "Itzawisis." There was a gate that opened to let us through, and then for some time we drove along what might have been the surface of the moon, for all the living things that broke the expanse of brownness separated from the scorching sky only by waves of heat that tormented the interloper with memories of iced drinks and blue swimming places.

All at once the African told us to stop. Nothing seemed very

different about the spot; there were a few thornbushes and
a dying brown tree in the distance. We turned the car around
so it would be facing out in case we had to get away quickly;
it got stuck, and not for the last time we were glad it was light
enough to lift.

Sherman and I left Emory at the wheel and followed the
African, apparently toward nothing in particular. The African
was too confused by circumstances or by language barriers to
make much sense, and we couldn't discover who or what we
would find and whether it or they would be transportable; so
we carried along the tape recorder and cameras, and must have
looked more like tourists nearing the Pyramids than people
who had come halfway around the world to meet a banished
minister.

Soon we were climbing slowly up a rise, and the African's
tension seemed to mount with the landscape. Then we came
to the top, and understood why: we stood now on a level place
higher than the surrounding countryside, and were visible to
anyone for miles around. In the distance were some huts, most
to our right but one to itself in the other direction. It was toward this one that we now hurried, as much as we could hurry
with all the equipment and after the long trudge through sands
eager to swallow our feet.

The hut we came to was made of sticks in the ground bound
together by canvas and topped by an intermittent roof that
shielded most of the inside from the sun. A dog and some
scrawny chickens had made peace with each other and stayed
close together in the shade. The African said: "Of course he
may not be here. We must hurry in any event."

Sherman dropped back to take pictures. A moment later a
man in a hat and tattered European clothing appeared in the
doorway. He was more bronze than black, his cheekbones set
high in the Nama manner under eyes that seemed almost to

slant. The face was a young face—at first I thought this an illusion caused by his hat, but it was not an illusion—warm and open, somehow striking; the first sight of it brought Harry Belafonte to mind.

The two Africans exchanged greetings in the clicking sounds of the Nama language, and then the man of the hut stepped forward.

My first words were not consciously a paraphrase, but I heard myself saying, "Pastor Kooper, I presume?"

His reply stretched the extraordinary moment so that it haunted the whole trip and has affected all the days since: "You are the men who have come all the way from America to help my people. It is wonderful that now in your country is a desire to help, for such help from America can mean freedom where now is only slavery."

The greetings exchanged, Markus Kooper said something in Nama, and vanished into the hut. The guide, who had been growing more and more jittery, now said, "Come, please; we must go quickly away," and trotted off in a direction not at all the one from which we had just come. Neither Sherman nor I could imagine what was upsetting him, and it seemed peculiar to dash off having just met Markus Kooper, but his agitation was so profound that we followed close behind.

"What about Markus Kooper?" I called.

"Soon, soon," he said, and we ran back by a route that seemed to double the distance to the car. Nor was the flight then finished; we must move the car, and he would explain as we went. And so he did, in a strange mixture of English and German, with much pointing and gesturing.

It was all a matter of the other huts, the ones that had been to the right when we had gone to the left. They were used by the administration, we slowly came to understand, to house men who spied on Markus Kooper.

"Markus may go nowhere without permission from the welfare commissioner," he said. "They watch from those places
so they may be paid if they catch him going."

Now we were to drive to a place where Markus Kooper could
meet us without going near the other huts. This avoiding of
the huts was also the reason for the circuitous return. The
guide was sure our coming away had not been noticed, but
of our approach and the meeting at the hut he was less optimistic. It particularly enraged him that there should be spies
so far away from everything; the Africans who brought provisions from time to time would have to be more careful.

We had reached a spot that satisfied the guide, and now we
sat and waited in the silence of the great cauterized void, and
grew tense from the unexplained delay. Why should it take
Markus Kooper so long to come? How long was it wise to sit
here? Wasn't it possible the welfare commissioner might appear?

"He comes every month, once," the guide said. "It is all
right to wait here." But there were signs of his earlier agitation
even as he spoke.

An hour passed, a sweaty nervous hour of great thirst and
imaginings. At last I decided there was nothing to do but go
all the way back to Pastor Kooper's hut. If it were unsafe to
drive, we could still walk, and walking could be no worse than
this interminable airless frying. The guide was opposed to the
idea. It could do no good: either there was trouble, in which
case to be there could only make matters worse; or there was
not, in which case Markus Kooper would be with us soon. I
had started from the car, and he was following to try to
dissuade me, when I saw an unfamiliar figure in clerical garb
hurrying toward us.

Then the figure was upon us, and it was Markus Kooper,
dignified and breathless.

"And now, please," he said, "shall we go to Hoachanas?"

The suggestion of going next to Hoachanas was at first a startling one. We were 150 miles away, and there was much we had planned to do before going so far to the north. Further, there was the complication of transporting a man illegally to a destination where his presence would constitute the gravest sort of offense.

It was the late afternoon of a Saturday. By morning Pastor Kooper could be with his congregation for services for the first time in five months. We deposited the guide in a safe spot, and set out by indirection for Hoachanas.

What followed was the most fruitful drive of the whole trip. We had a remarkable man to ourselves for many hours—a man of great sweetness and patience, and of a courage so luminous it was contagious; a man who knew the lives and hopes of his people as few men can know such things. From him we learned the story of the Rooie Nasie tribe, and saw the miseries of a suffering people through eyes that had lost none of their gentleness for all the torment they had witnessed. First he talked of history.

"Hoachanas is a place which was found by the Nama people called the Rooie Nasie about the year 1700. From that time up to now the generations of Rooie Nasie people have been residing at Hoachanas. Hoachanas is and has been always the headquarters of the Rooie Nasie people. When the Reserve was proclaimed, it was proclaimed as a 50,000-hectare Reserve by the German Government. And no portion of the 50,000 hectare of land has afterward been sold or given to any white man, but the Union Government has took 36,000 hectares of the land and given it to the white people."

We asked about the statements of the South African Government that they wished to move the people from Hoachanas for their own good because they would have twice as much land at Itzawisis.

"You have seen this Itzawisis," he said. "Can you believe people shall exist in such a place where there is not a drop of water?" He told of the drilling of many boreholes, only two of which had yielded any water, and this water had been condemned as unfit for human consumption "even by the man in Pretoria. If what they wish is to help my people, why do they not give back the land they have stolen from us at Hoachanas?"

Then we asked about his own deportation, and he told us a story we were to hear confirmed by many witnesses in Hoachanas:

"In the early morning of the 29th of January, the magistrate of Rehoboth, accompanied by a colonel and about thirty men, came to Hoachanas and the magistrate called me and told me that they came to remove me from Hoachanas. I asked him whether they came to remove only me or whether they have come to remove all of us. The colonel said that they came to remove me today, but if I want to do so I can tell the others that they too will be removed. So I go to my house and I was putting on my church uniform.

"While I was busy putting on my uniform, the people came from their houses to take up the place in front of my house. They say the police will not take me away. They said that I am a minister and I am in no way responsible for their refusal to move from Hoachanas. It is then the colonel ordered the police to fight the people. So the police fight the people so that the blood was running down the bodies of the people. I was then fetched and thrown into the lorry.

"When I was removed from my place at Hoachanas I had absolutely not a spoonful of mealie meal to quieten my children if they will cry from hunger. Nor have I anything to give them to comfort them, but the officer just threw me away there in the desert with my family and all."

The drive itself had its share of misfortunes, and at least twice it seemed certain we would be intercepted before we could deliver Markus Kooper to Hoachanas. He has since escaped across the Kalahari to New York and the U.N., where he is now beyond the reach of the South African police. But most of the people who made it possible for us to complete the journey from Itzawisis to Hoachanas are still in South West; and it is not easy to tell of rescues without giving clues that may jeopardize the rescuers. One may refer to anonymous Africans in nameless towns who concealed strangers at a critical moment, but if one grows more specific one risks the well-being of those who did so much, asking only that they not be betrayed in return.

There are no courtroom proceedings for someone suspected of such activities; there are only the sudden appearance of the police, and then the beatings, and then the disappearance of another "agitator." And how convenient to the needs of a police state are the pass laws and the economic stringencies that girdle each African movement with illegalities, and make conspicuous those who have more than the customary resources! Was there an African driving a truck on a Sunday in August in the vicinity of Uhlenhorst? Check the records—there can't be more than two Kaffirs in the whole area who have trucks. Was an African in the streets of Otjiwarongo after dark? Check the records—there can't be half a dozen who have had exemptions from the curfew.

Was there a kindly, nonpolitical missionary somewhere along the way who, as his religion teaches, took in from the freezing night men of different races? Was there such a man who, asking no questions, fed and sheltered these strangers that they might be spared the cruelty of the desert winter until they could again go on their way? If such a thing happened and if such a man exists, he can be found; and who will believe (or care) that he did not know what his guests were doing?

It is not a thing to do lightly, to violate the law by housing people overnight without permits, to say nothing of feeding black men and white at the same table. Troublemaking missionaries who do such things are usually foreigners, and foreigners need visas, and the government need explain to no one if it refuses or cancels a troublemaking foreigner's visa.

At last it was Sunday morning, and after the endless dust there came an astonishing sight. To our right was a steeple, presiding over a countryside whose barrenness gave way now to patches of greenness; in the shade of palm trees cattle were drinking from a natural watering place. This was Hoachanas, and we were in time for Markus Kooper to appear at services in the simple church that had been his ministry for so many years. There were some in the congregation who at first thought his appearance a dream, and others who at first thought it a miracle; but there were none who did not rejoice in it, and the feeling of the people for this man was a lovely thing to see.

We left Markus Kooper at his church and drove some miles away to a hidden place where we expected to record the statements of a few of the leaders of Hoachanas. There came instead a great outpouring of people filled with things they wished to say. Markus Kooper's presence was a crime against the state, but he went among them, translating, clarifying, explaining, soothing; some spoke in Afrikaans and some in the Nama language, but all told of the love of the people for their homes and their land, and of their pride in the church they had built with their own hands and pennies.

There was much talk about the bitter events of the 29th of January, when the police had arrived to deport Markus Kooper, people said, and "we were made to see our blood run down on the ground." One man told of his wife who miscarried after she had been "bodily assaulted," and as he spoke of her he wept and shook his fist. Then he bared an injured leg and waved a bandaged arm at the tape recorder, as if to be sure the evidence of his wounds was noted in the recording.

All afternoon rugged men held off or yielded to tears of frustration and spread out the sadness of their lives:

"I am weaker than a child because I cannot even provide for my children and my wife like a father ought to."

"Our minister, the person to whom we looked up as a leader, he has been taken away from us, has been thrown into a truck like a thief and taken away."

There was an eagerness to the telling and a gratitude that someone would listen that swelled into a notion that help would soon be on its way. But all afternoon there hovered over men ashamed of being always afraid the fear that the police would come upon them while we taped their words in the bright sunlight: "We are expecting these bearers of death to turn up here at any minute—we are waiting their rearrival every day."

They spoke of the brutality of the police from a neighboring village called Derm:

"These police come to Hoachanas without asking any questions; they run into our houses and just do what he is wanting to do in our houses. He doesn't even ask anything; just ran in to our houses and say he is searching after the beer; but he is actually not searching after the beer."

"We non-Europeans meet the police of the Derm station, then it is just as good if we meet the death itself. The first thing that he will do is ask me the pass; if he finds me without a pass I must be arrested and bound and thrown in the lorry. With my best knowledge I know that this country belongs to me and I must go quite freely in this country wherever I want to go."

The frightened copper faces of the Rooie Nasie seemed that afternoon the universal face of those who suffer and have always suffered, and are forgotten in the timelessness of their misery. The eyes were the bewildered eyes of a wearied peasantry asking help against those whose greed seems to feed on the hunger of others, asking why men who have so much begrudge even scraps to those who have so little.

These men could be Chinese or Spaniards or Slavs or sharecroppers in Alabama, I thought, but they are not. They are wards of mankind, and they are in an international territory, and they suffer not because they are peasants but because they are not white. And what Civilization ought to do for the downtrodden everywhere it must do for these who are not only its wards but its victims.

The words of Mburumba and Jane Kerina were much in mind when we left Markus Kooper and drove away from Hoachanas. How much had happened in the long day that began at Itzawisis! We had learned something about the reliability of pronouncements by the South African Government; but more rewarding was the change in the spirits of the people of Hoachanas. Now the beloved man who was their minister was with them again, at least for the moment, and he had returned with men who had come a long distance to hear their story and who promised to go long distances to tell of it; and something close to hope whispered through the remnants of this place that had so long been home to these beleaguered people.

We did not know until Markus Kooper's arrival in New York that the police from Derm had appeared in Hoachanas less than three minutes after we had departed.

VI Soon after the trip to Hoachanas we visited the
Etosha Pan, which is the major game reserve in the
Territory. Here, in the far northern reaches of the
Police Zone, is one of those natural havens that crops up so
unexpectedly out of arid wilderness; here water collects so
that animals may exist, and the white man rules himself off
limits and protects the beasts with a solicitude denied to other
human beings.

The drought that had parched South West for four years had
withered even the Pan, but there were still watering places and
a great variety of game that made it a place of wonder and
beauty to us. The unpremeditated cruelties of the lower orders
seemed somehow mild compared to the deliberate plunder organized by superior brains a few miles to the north or south.
It was an almost physical relief to be away from the endless
dust and the needless suffering; and to watch families of elegant
and placid giraffes, and the parade of Thomson's gazelles
and dik-diks (the chihuahuas of the species) and kudu and
wildebeeste (the gnus of crossword-puzzle fame) and spring-
bok, the lilting tawny animal that is South Africa's national
mascot.

At last great clumping elephants appear—far off at first; but
we wait, motionless behind our cameras, hoping to catch a
touch of the majesty of the moment. Soon a mammoth wrinkled
hulk is foolishly near, and we watch the improbable winding
nose as it sucks up sustenance and feeds the inaccessible mouth;

until all at once a shift of wind brings news of our presence,
and not knowing that we stand close to admire and not to hunt,
he fears, and fearing, becomes a foe. And so we are left to
wonder at the inability of man to communicate with others of
God's creatures, and, more mysterious yet, with himself; and
turn at last to go.

Just across the northern boundary of the Pan lies Ovamboland, an area that exists in almost total isolation from the outside world. In John Gunther's words, "The northern areas of
South West are the most 'closed' part of Africa. The official in
charge of the South West African administration told us that
even he could not give permission for anybody to enter the
north. Authority has to come all the way from Pretoria." *

There, in conditions of rural poverty made unbearable by
the endless drought, live perhaps a quarter of a million Africans, the main source of labor for the white man in the Territory. It is in Ovamboland that the quasi-official South West
Africa Native Labor Association does its recruiting: Sign here
(a thumbprint will do) or starve. Go to the Police Zone to
work, or watch your children scrabble for weeds in the dust.

You are free to go or not to go, so it is not slavery that
you will have no say about who your employer is or what
kind of work you will do; or that you may not quit if you are
mistreated, or for any other reason until your contract has
been worked through; or that you may not bring your wife
along, or organize to seek better working conditions, or rise
above the most menial of tasks; or that you will be paid $7
a month, unless your employer docks you for "damages" to
other parts of his property.

Still, it's better than not eating at all. And once you're in
the Police Zone a miracle may happen—perhaps a kindly

* Strictly speaking the Administrator of South West Africa can give such
permission, but this appears to be done only under the most unusual circumstances.

white man will pay more than the contract requires, or perhaps somehow something may be done to change the order of things. Nothing can be done in Ovamboland, where virtually every white is a militiaman of one sort or another, and where the response to vaulting African discontent has been a police rule uninterrupted even by the scruples of occasional legalistic Europeans and unmodified by concern about the writings of the itinerant journalists who plague the government periodically in less remote places.

I once discussed the contract labor system with a distinguished English-speaking lawyer who was irritated that I thought it close to slavery. I asked him what term he would use if he were bound on pain of criminal sanctions by a contract he couldn't read to work for an employer he couldn't select for twenty cents a day. "Of course," he said, "it would be slavery if it were done to whites. But these people don't know anything different. They're satisfied—grateful for the most part—or they wouldn't come. Nobody ropes them in, you know."

A flow of such offhand remarks by Europeans confirmed African grievances about their treatment at the hands of their employers. Several times white farmers told us, as horse trainers might chuckle over a trade secret, that they did not have to worry about their Kaffirs getting cheeky if they just beat them now and then. But apparently beatings are not always enough.

Mrs. Emil Appolus was a staff nurse in the non-European hospital in Keetmanshoop before she fled the country. The following incident is not unrepresentative of her testimony before the South West Africa Committee of the United Nations:

"One day while I was working in the hospital four contract labourers were brought in, all from the same farm. They had gunshot wounds and were bleeding. We were shocked and asked the Medical Superintendent what the matter was. His explanation was, 'Oh you know, these Ovambos are very stupid. They happen to have run into some jackal trap and that is how they got shot.'

"As I got acquainted with the patients later I found out the reason why these men had sustained their injuries. Some sheep were missing from the farm where they worked as herds-boys. The farmer got them together and started beating them with a *sjambok* [leather whip]. They tried to run away and were chased by the farmer and his two sons in a motor van. They had guns and shot at the men when they would not stop running. One of them died on the farm. They could not tell me what happened to him and he was never brought in the hospital.

"I went to the Superintendent's office and told him what I had heard. He told me not to worry as these Ovambos are all liars. I could do nothing, but wept."

There are some masters who treat their servants as they might treat household pets who must do the master's bidding but for whom there grows an affection that may inspire kind-ness and bring rewards. But more commonly the attitude of whites toward blacks is something beyond hate, something at once more cruel and less understandable, something like their attitude toward insects that are to be tolerated until they get in the way and then are to be driven off or crushed, whichever is less trouble. Rare indeed is the white man who is willing to accept the fact that his servants are human beings who think and resent and suffer—and who one day soon will *plan*.

We heard many stories like the one told us by an eminent clergyman about a devout parishioner, a well-to-do farmer who had been driving an open truck loaded with African workers. The branch of a tree struck one of the Africans and did serious harm to his eye, but the farmer saw no reason to make a special trip to town, and when the African finally managed to get medical treatment it was too late to save the eye. The clergyman, perhaps spurred on by some vague biblical parallel, asked if the African couldn't have been taken to a doctor sooner, a question, he said, that seemed to astonish the farmer, who explained that the Bible applied to relationships between human beings: "You're not fool enough to think the bloody Kaffirs have feelings like you and I do!"

"If he was trying to conceal from me his real attitude toward blacks, I can only say he had succeeded in concealing it from himself in the process," the clergyman said. "Like so many others, he is sincere in his belief that divine Providence intended the black man to shiver through life, and furthermore that the black man is content to do so. I have hoped this attitude is a veneer, a convenient rationalization to minimize guilt and to smother kindly instincts and the pull of Christian teachings. But if it is a veneer, those who wear it are so used to seeing themselves in it that they are no longer aware of it." Nor, it might be added, are their victims.

The sort of interracial friendships that ignore government and custom alike in South Africa are absent in South West. Even the personal warmth that perseveres between many masters and their servants in the Union is an infrequent phenomenon here.

There are, of course, many Europeans who are distressed at what they see going on around them. A few—the staffs of some non-European hospitals, for instance—do their best to ease the situation. A substantial number are more dismayed by what they feel are likely to be the ultimate consequences of such attitudes than they are by the attitudes themselves, but the futility and injudiciousness of speaking out are potent incentives to silence. Not the least useful of the by-products of mounting external pressures are the excuse and encouragement these pressures provide for this minority European viewpoint to make itself heard.

For years the occasional voices of dissent among whites were invariably those of missionaries whose outspokenness increased the precariousness of their work. The government grew first weary and then frightened of clerical criticism, and decided to force mission schools to follow apartheid practices and use the official syllabuses that provide an education tailored to the theories of white supremacy. Missions have been subjected to harassing regulations that govern a mass of trivia, including such matters as who may visit overnight. Sermons are audited; and nonconforming clergymen have been banished or warned about their visas or passports.

Such actions flout the special guarantees of the Mandatory treaty protecting freedom of religion and assuring missionaries of unrestricted access to the Territory. We said in summary at the U.N.: "The ban on Father Scott is not exceptional in its violation of the letter and the spirit of the Mandate Agreement; fear and repression are the rule among all religious groups except the one upon which the government smiles. . . .

"It may indicate how grave is the fear of government reprisal, and thus how absent the atmosphere of religious freedom evoked by the Mandate Agreement, to report that time and again we had to promise not to cite names, places, or even denominations, before missionaries would agree to talk candidly with us about their problems and hopes."

Perhaps nothing that happened while we were in South West so dramatized the chasm between the world of the white man and that of the black as a by-election for a seat in the Provincial Assembly that took place in the Mariental district. The Nationalist party of South West had won the seat in 1955, but not overwhelmingly, and the Opposition had hopes of reversing the result.

The campaign was spirited, and aroused much interest

among Europeans. Everyone speculated about the effect of the
bolt of Mr. Japie Basson, an M.P. from South West who had
quit the Nationalist party, and argued about how the pivotal
German vote would go. Newspapers gave a good deal of space
to charges and countercharges. Expert political correspondents
were flown in from Cape Town and Johannesburg. Special
broadcasts were scheduled, and up and down the countryside
betting flared and tempers rose. A detached observer might
have wondered what all the fuss was about, but there could
be no doubt that almost every white in the Territory felt personally involved. It became very hard to remember that the
whole uproar involved a grand total of less than fifteen hundred votes.

Election Day dawned in a flurry of predictions and inter-
pretative warnings, and the results created great excitement in
sophisticated circles in Windhoek. The Nationalists had held
the seat, but their margin had been reduced by about fifty
votes in the process—a switch of sufficient consequence to
shake the European community. Headlines and analyses filled
the newspapers the following day, when it happened that I had
to go into a Location for a meeting.

For all its impact there, the election might have occurred
in pre-Aztec Mexico. No one seemed aware that a political
event of apparently enormous importance had just taken place
around the corner. I remarked that the Europeans had held a
heated election in Mariental, and asked if anyone would be
interested in seeing the returns. There was a puzzled silence,
and then one man said, "Oh yes, I almost forgot—the Europeans have been arguing about whose foot is to be closest on
our necks."

Then a large gentle-faced fellow whom I knew to be a
teacher in a mission school spoke, and the tone was one of
reproach: "It is hard not to be resentful of such elections as

these," he said, "but it is foolish to pretend it does not matter who wins them. It may not matter in any way that can bring cheer to the people, but it will make much difference in the way the fight will have to be conducted."

There was no real conflict between the two statements: the foot would in any case be close on the neck, but in the strange Alice-in-Wonderland world of South African politics, even the inflated little by-election in Mariental had significance.

There has been as little difference between the racial policies of the dominant white political parties in South West as in the Union; small wonder that to Africans the electoral processes are not only an affront but a bore. There are, however, differences in European opinion about the relationship of South West to the Union.

Afrikaners who have recently moved to South West generally assume that the Territory is, or at least should be and soon will be, a fifth province of the Union. Such notions are not popular among other European groups. Events are sharpening this disagreement with unexpected speed.

The encouragement of immigration from South Africa since the war has swelled the Afrikaner community until it comprises about half the European total, and approximately two-thirds of the whites now resident in South West are in fact South African citizens. Most Afrikaners support the Nationalist party, which favors what amounts to *de facto* integration. But now even Nationalists play down the "fifth province" talk and are uncomfortable about pronouncements by high officials in Cape Town and Pretoria who have boasted publicly about the eventual incorporation of South West into the Union.

The chief rival of the Nationalists, the United National South West party, scenting a horse that can be flogged into life, warns constantly about hidden assimilation if the Nationalists are kept in power. It is this issue—or the issue of whether this is an issue—that stirs emotions and sways elections more than any other.

Despite the recent influx of Afrikaners from the Union, it is likely that a majority of whites in South West still oppose annexation. Their reasons vary, and are rarely related to any of the problems that bedevil Africans and engage the attention of so many people at the U.N. Nevertheless, many whites privately welcome the agitation at the U.N. All the talk about mandates and international status, if not an unmixed blessing, has its uses in stalling off an integration that could jeopardize South West's lenient tax structures and tie her buoyant economy to the more splotchy prospects of the Union.

Furthermore, the German element fears its language rights would not survive in a "fifth province," despite repeated official assurances; and there is a sort of nostalgic hankering for an independent *white* South West Africa among early colonizers and their descendants.

A lingering bitterness against the Smuts Government for having interned German males during World War II has kept the bulk of the German vote in the Nationalist column to date, in spite of the denials of leaders of UNSWP that their party is connected with the United party of South Africa. But resentment is rising against the tightening of links to the Union, and old hates are now balanced by new fears. The last thing the German wants is "his" country turned over to black rule by some international agency, and it seems to him more and more likely that this is precisely where Nationalist policies are leading.

Thus the feeling grows among the Germans that the English may be snobs but they are not fools. If this attitude crystallizes, much of the German swing vote may be lost to the Nationalists, and with it their narrow majority.

It is precisely to voters in this unhappy predicament of

choosing between unpleasant memories and uninviting prospects that Japie Basson's new National Union (which calls itself the "South West party" in South West) seeks especially
to appeal. The National Union sees itself as a political force
capable of uniting Afrikaners, British, and Germans who are
ready to forget ancient squabbles in the interests of a sort of
white popular front. Basson, himself an Afrikaner, has gone
about the countryside warning that South Africa has "not a
single friend in the world" and that as a result of Nationalist
policies the Afrikaner has become the "most hated tribe in the
world." He hopes to split other "moderate" Afrikaners away
from the *laager* mentality of the Nationalist party, and if such
a split should ultimately occur, Basson may be received as
its prophet or reviled as its cause. He did not contest his seat
in the 1961 elections but was returned to Parliament from a
safe United party constituency in Johannesburg as part of the
electoral entente formed by the United party and the National
Union. He thus retains a vote in Parliament, but his absence
from the affairs of the Territory will remove a cogent and
relatively forward-looking voice from a place where it is sorely
needed.

The international reaction to Sharpeville and the increasing
turmoil in the Portuguese colonies have ricocheted into white
thinking in South West. Solid commercial figures find it unreasonable and unpalatable that they may be caught up willy-
nilly in a boycott of Union goods. And there is a grudging
awareness that embittered black revolts in South Africa and
Angola will not be confined by artificial borders.

More and more Europeans in South West are beginning to
suspect that apartheid has been a needless invitation to disaster:
segregation and tacit white supremacy would have continued
indefinitely in any case, but the world-wide revulsion against

apartheid can be fatal to both segregation and South Africa;
and thus apartheid is not merely bad politics but lunacy.

In fact, a broad spectrum of non-Nationalist thinking may
be moving at last toward more moderate racial policies.
The chairman of UNSWP astounded the country when he returned from a trip abroad with baleful prophecies about the
future of European civilization in South West if drastic changes
were not made forthwith. Perhaps even more remarkable is
an essay published recently by one of the leading advocates in
South West, Mr. Isidor Goldblatt, Q.C., of Windhoek. Mr.
Goldblatt is careful not to espouse an overtly nonracial program, but the tenor of his conclusions is clear in these excerpts
from his pamphlet:

"Frank recognition must be given to the fact that in South
West Africa the African will have to be developed under the
Trusteeship System to a stage where he can share in political
responsibility according to the importance of his numbers. The
Administering Authority and the whites in the Territory will,
however, have to make a genuine effort to develop the African
as rapidly as possible and in such a manner as to gain his confidence. . . . What should be realized is this: that the choice
for the white man is not between continuing to enjoy his present privileged position and sharing of responsibility with the
Africans. No, the choice is between sharing responsibility
through orderly development, and being swept away altogether
by hostile and uncontrolled African forces, who will be in no
mood to extend liberal treatment to those who refuse to extend
that treatment to the African. And it is precisely through the
United Nations that the necessary controlled development can
take place."

Indeed, the Nationalists themselves have not been entirely
immune to the sweep of events. Many have modified their at-

titude toward the U.N., or at least have reviewed the tactics
they would use in dealing with the fact of rising external interest. The mayor of Windhoek has gone so far as to announce
that he would "welcome" a visit by the South West Africa
Committee of the U.N., despite the fact that the South African
Government has barred the committee from the Union as well
as from South West. The mayor believes that the committee
would find Africans generally content if it came to South
West, and that to allow legal quibbles to keep the committee
out is to court heightened international antagonism where
otherwise it might be eased.

UNSWP and the National Union do not appear to differ
very substantially on current major issues, and it may be
doubted that two opposition parties saying much the same
thing will unify rather than split the non-Nationalist vote, even
when they agree not to oppose one another in specific electoral
contests. Nonetheless the combined strength of the European
opposition seems to be rising in South West, and may soon be
sufficient to end Nationalist control of the Provincial Assembly.

Whether such a change would make any difference in the
status of non-Europeans is not clear. It is clear, however, that
no program yet contemplated by any Europeans in South West
represents an ultimate solution that would be acceptable to
nonwhites. Even Advocate Goldblatt's proposals—courageous
and farsighted though they be—are couched in terms designed
to convince the white electorate that many of their privileges
can best be preserved by accepting U.N. Trusteeship. This may
be a sensible approach to the white electorate, but it is not a
very effective inducement to African trust. And it will be particularly difficult to gain African trust in a country where white
indifference to nonwhite thinking has been so nearly unanimous
that there has never been a liberal white community or even an

active nonpolitical group seeking to communicate across racial barriers.

There is another factor in European politics that deserves notice. Many whites in South West do not like the way the present government runs things in the *Union;* otherwise sentiment for at least some sort of federation might well be overwhelming. The withdrawal from the Commonwealth has reinforced an impression that the South African ship of state is unmoored and anchorless, a floating madhouse floundering in a minefield; and there is no eagerness to be aboard when the explosion occurs.

There is also foreboding that even if such a debacle is not imminent, South Africa is becoming increasingly a police state for Europeans as well as for non-Europeans; and there is little enthusiasm for getting more deeply immured in a Union-style situation where the individual liberties of whites keep vanishing in the sacred name of keeping down blacks. This has already begun to happen, as we reported at the U.N.:

"This police state atmosphere in South West is insinuating itself into the lives of the European population as well. . . . It will be said that few Europeans disagree fundamentally with present racial policies; we would observe only that we encountered such Europeans, and that their hesitancy to speak out, and their fear of being quoted, betray an unhappy erosion of traditional freedoms within the limited European community."

All in all, a combination of circumstances is tending to produce a paradox that finds South West Europeans, whose racial attitudes are if anything harsher than those of their counterparts in the Union, taking a far more conciliatory line than those counterparts toward the U.N. This line could lead to a significantly more liberal approach to the problems of nonwhites, even as it could to intramural clashes with the Union

Government. It is usually anticipated that a hostile ruling by the World Court would serve to unify all Europeans behind the intransigent position of the South African Government, but it is at least possible that the long-run effect of such a ruling would be the opposite. Not a few South Westers have begun to suspect that polite bows in the direction of change may serve the *status quo* better than defiant postures and doctrinaire rhetoric.

Organized political activity among Africans is an innovation in South West, one that the government has done its best to discourage and stamp out. Especially in rural areas loyalties still tend to be tribal, but a more general sense of identification with other black men, and particularly with other black men who live in South West, is growing. Tribal chiefs who have stood firm against the government have been able to maintain a good deal of respect and support from their people. Where they have not done so their authority has been challenged by less traditional forces.

The German wars and South African ruthlessness crushed much of the individual black man's resistance, if none of his resentment. Now once more resistance is stirring, and a handful of younger leaders is trying to mobilize a fight in the pattern of the African nationalist movements; but it is extremely difficult for a non-European to attain national prominence.

For one thing, the government, despite the injunctions of the Mandate, does everything it can to prevent non-European leadership from developing. Anyone who shows signs of capacity and instinct for leadership invites banishment or jail. Chiefs who rejected the Bantu Authorities Act are restricted to small areas and threatened with deposition.

The names of the men who have been petitioning at the U.N. are known and respected among Africans; and in urban areas the elected members of Location Advisory Councils often acquire considerable local stature. But only Hosea Kutako, the Paramount Chief of the Hereros, has overcome problems of communication and tribal barriers to achieve a national following; and he is now ninety-one years old. Everywhere we went there was a veneration for this man that exceeded even our expectations from what we had heard and read in New York.

Such is Chief Kutako's eminence that the government has not been able to silence him and has not dared to depose or deport him. It is Chief Kutako who has set much of the tone of the African opposition since World War II. He is a devout Christian, a disciple of nonviolence who once studied for the ministry; and he has insisted that change must come through action by the United Nations. If Hosea Kutako's efforts do not produce results, it is unlikely that his successors will wish, much less be able, to restrain Africans indefinitely from less gentle tactics in the seeking of freedom.

Two African political groups, the South West Africa People's Organization and the South West Africa National Union, have appeared within the past few years. Both decry tribal divisions and assert goals similar to those of the African National Congress and the Pan Africanist Congress in South Africa. Unhappily the similarity seems destined to extend to the working relationship between the two organizations; already there are signs of serious friction. SWAPO grew out of the Ovamboland People's Organization, but both organizations are still young and are handicapped in their work by a lack of experienced personnel, as well as by the customary government repressions.

Perhaps the most blatant expression of the government's intentions for the future of non-Europeans in South West is to be found in its education policies.

There are of course no facilities for higher education for
nonwhites in South West, and it is now against government
policy to allow Africans from the Territory to study even at an
African "tribal college" in the Union. Only one non-European
has ever been granted permission to accept a scholarship offered him at a university outside South Africa. And as of the
time of our visit to South West only two Africans—the two
whom we had met in New York—had ever received under-
graduate degrees.

Just as striking an indication of government policy is its
failure to provide an adequate elementary-school system. In
1959—in the fortieth year of the Mandate—there was a grand
total of 9,969 Africans in all schools in the Police Zone, of
whom 8,884 were in mission schools and only 367 were above
the equivalent of fifth grade. Not a single African had passed
beyond fifth grade in the area outside the Police Zone, nor was
there a nonwhite anywhere in the Territory studying beyond
eleventh grade.

At least 70 per cent of the total budget for education is
regularly allocated to the 10 per cent of the population that is
white; the remainder must cover all nonwhite education, including expenditures for Coloured schools and assistance to mission
schools.

In the whole of the Territory there is only one government
school for Africans that offers classes beyond fifth grade. This is
the training school in Okahandja, whose graduates supply the
bulk of teachers for the rest of the government's African
schools. Thus all nonwhite education outside the Police Zone,
and the overwhelming share of it within the Zone as well, has
been left to the churches. But now mission schools have been
placed under restrictions so severe that the churches have not
always agreed how to react. Some have felt it inadmissible to
maintain schools on an apartheid basis using government sylla-

buses; others see no sense in closing down most of what little opportunity for education is available to African children, and have continued to function as best they can.

Africans and church officials have mixed feelings about the whole situation. Emory, Sherman, and I were later caught up in a dispute at the U.N. over which basic policy—to keep schools open under apartheid or to close them entirely—is the more desirable. In the end, perhaps the critical point to bear in mind is that the villain is neither a church that decides to keep its schools open under protest nor Africans who may object to this decision, but the government that imposes such choices in the first place.

Those schools that do stay open must increasingly conform to the views of South Africa's Minister of Native Affairs about what is suitable for Africans to learn. A Commission of Enquiry into Non-European Education recommended in November, 1959, that all "native" education in South West be modeled on the system already in force in the Union. Course work should consist of such items as handicrafts, nature study, hygiene, and religion.

Even when more academic subjects are taught, they become funnels for government propaganda. Hans had spent some time teaching in a Coloured primary school. He described this experience as follows:

"In the school textbooks our children have always to read their own people being referred to by derogatory terms. We have to teach our children how the brave white man has blazed forth with Bible and gun against our own savage ancestors. The textbooks carefully avoid mention that there might be a different interpretation of the conflicts of the past. It is not considered safe for a student to mention this in his examinations. . . . Apartheid education is intended to isolate nonwhites from cultural contact and influence from the rest of the world."

Thus if an elementary course in geography is offered, it is likely to center upon a study of the street arrangements in a Location; and instruction in languages is molded to minimize awareness of events beyond the most parochial. English, for instance, is continually downgraded. "This proceeds," we reported at the U.N., "in the face of the theoretically bilingual nature of the Mandatory Power, and is not slowed down in the least by the earnest wish of many Africans to learn English as a lingua franca and as a vehicle for communication with the outside world."

The 1960 report of the U.N. Committee on South West Africa summarized its study of non-European educational opportunities as follows: "Beyond some minor teaching and menial positions at the lowest levels, their [Africans'] training and education seems directed merely to preparing the 'Natives' as a source of cheap labor for the benefit of the 'Europeans.' The Committee considers that as far as the 'Native' and 'Coloured' population of the Territory are concerned, the basic ills of administration stem directly or indirectly from the rigid enforcement of the policy of apartheid based on the concept of white supremacy over all other races."

Thus very few Africans have an opportunity to learn a European language. And since we knew only a smattering of words in any of the tribal tongues, there was a constant need for interpreters.

Many of the Africans who do speak some English or German are hired by the government to translate in courts or police stations, or to perform other official functions. At first we shied away from using government employees, but this proved an unnecessary precaution. Our contacts knew if someone were not to be trusted.

It is a remarkable indication of sentiment about the government that none of the countless Africans whom we met, or even of that vast additional number who must have known what we were doing, informed on us, although this could easily have been done anonymously and with handsome reward.

There were times, however, when finding reliable interpreters was a problem. During several slow-moving recording sessions we suggested that translation be dispensed with, to save time. On one occasion this suggestion seemed to perplex the Africans even after we had explained that someone could be found to do the translating in London or New York. Finally one said: "I can believe there is a machine which can understand English. But can there really be such a machine that understands Herero?"

What proved to be our most difficult experience with language barriers came midway through the stay in South West. We were to meet with a group of chiefs by daylight, which meant heightened pressures for speed and a generally tense afternoon at best. An obliging young fellow had volunteered in broken English to translate for us, and for lack of an alternative we had accepted his offer. There had been others who at first had seemed painfully unsure of their English, but who had performed almost fluently once recording was under way.

He remained largely silent on the way to meet the chiefs, which we assumed meant he wished to rest before the impending mental exertions. When he did speak up, it was usually to give directions or to repeat a number of phrases that seemed to have something to do with problems confronting sheep during an extended drought.

Eventually we arrived at the hideaway where the chiefs awaited us. The usual hearty greetings were exchanged without much need for specific translating. Sherman set up the taping apparatus; Emory found a perch from which to watch for any hint of approaching dust; and we all settled down to record the statements of a battery of indignant men hardly able to contain their impatience to tell the world everything.

This they set out to do in a flood of words that seemed unrelieved by periods or even commas, and as the unintelligible eloquence cascaded out I wondered how we would ever get everything into English. The translator was looking more and more unhappy, and finally I decided I would have to break in, disrespectful though I felt in doing so.

Gestures that in my experience had come to mean "slow down" seemed to have the opposite effect in this instance, but at length I managed to extricate the machine from the chiefs and hand it over for translation. For a breathless moment there was total silence while the translator scratched his head and looked generally miserable. Then, as if the words might well be his last, he shouted into the microphone, "We beg U.N.O.: Help!"

I assumed the logjam had at last been broken and details would now be forthcoming, but after another awkward pause the machine was passed back to the chiefs, who doubtless resumed saying whatever it was they had been saying before. This time the most voluble of the chiefs accompanied his oral efforts with a great deal of agitated gesturing, and presently he raised three fingers, one by one, until they too were flailing away in untranslated fury. I was sure we were being given a three-point program, or a list of three major grievances, or perhaps three important details of local history.

Again there was some difficulty halting the oratory long enough to give English a chance. The interpreter was looking even more ill at ease; he kept scratching at his head as if it had become the nesting place of a whole swamp of mosquitos. The lifting of the microphone to his mouth seemed to exhaust him, but finally it was done; whereupon he froze completely. His mouth opened, nothing came out, and then it closed.

I waited lest more words merely add to his confusion; still

nothing came out. At last I said slowly, trying to sound very calm and patient and hoping to drown out the chiefs, who had resumed making urgent noises: "Don't worry about details. Just give us the key points of what has been said."

There was another pause, and then, as if torn from his brain in its final agony, there erupted a piercing cry: "We beg U.N.O.: Help, *Help, HELP!*"—and with each successive "Help" a finger flew up, till there were three waving and pointing accusingly at us, or maybe at the world all around us. And that was all.

We were able to have the recording of that afternoon translated more fully when we got back to New York, and it had been, as we suspected, an unusually informative discussion. But when all was said and done, no rendition of the most fervent message could have been more faithful to its spirit than the first: "We beg U.N.O.: Help, *Help, HELP!*"

For such is the cry that singes the soul of this troubled land. We heard it until we could never forget its sound in Nama, Ovambo, Herero, Damara, English, and even in Afrikaans— heard it said as a supplication, a reproof, a hope: Surely the great men and the great countries that are U.N.O. will help us, we who are their children, who have suffered so much, who have nowhere else to turn.

"I am Taseb speaking now. We are waiting from the United Nations very earnestly their help. We ask the Organization of the World Government to come and see the difficulties we are suffering each. And we ask the United Nations Organization to remove the Union Government and to place South West Africa under the trusteeship of the United Nations."

"I am the Chief, Hendrik Samuel Witbooi, of the Nama tribe. How much do we desire a chief of this country . . . to come personally to the country of America and to tell of our troubles to the United Nations. But until today we have been refused and will never be permitted to go over to New York.

"We have understood the United Nations Organization to be a dignified organization, which will see that all the people on the face of this earth will have their rights and freedom. It is therefore all of us, the chiefs of this country, request: that this country of ours be placed under the trusteeship of the United Nations Organization. Then we believe that we will become free."

"My name is Reverend Daniel Dausab: I have been waiting all the time upon men who will come from the United Nations Organization. The onliest thing we are getting is slavery. I will therefore wait on the help of the United Nations before I die. I also ask the United Nations that the Reverend Michael Scott be bringed back by the Administration of South West Africa."

"I am Evangelist Jonas Nakom: It was our wish to come to the United Nations Organization to tell there our feelings; personally and from face to face. We ask that the United Nations would see that we get back that land which was stolen by the Union Government.

"It would be better for the United Nations Organization not to be hindered by the actions of the delegation of the Union Government. Even if Mr. Eric Louw, as he usually did, take his hat and go out from the United Nations Organization the South West Africa Administration must be placed under the United Nations Organization."

"I Johannes Kubas: The Government under whom I am living today, who is boss over me, that is responsible for everything, that Government is my enemy . . . and I am asking for help please. . . . Here I am living so badly that I really do not know why I am still alive. If the Lord was not there then I would have been gone long ago. . . . The dogs of white men live ten times better than I do. . . .

"And I am asking the Lord that he should today please, please, place South West Africa under the hands of the United Nations. If the United Nations do not help us quickly we will die out like grass that has burn out. Our Fathers, please hear us and please help us. . . . I am praying the United Nations to dry my tears for me."

"The dogs of white men live ten times better than I do." The words haunted me, and I thought of the little girl in a European ghetto two decades ago sobbing to her mother that she wished she were a dog because the guards didn't beat the dogs. And now here, again, so soon, were human beings envying the lot of dogs.

VII There was one European in South West Africa who knew of our activities. We shall call this man Jan Meyer. His connection with us was a fact known to no one else. He was to leave South West from Windhoek a day and a half sooner than I, and we hoped to get there in time to report to him.

A meeting with Chief Hosea Kutako had been arranged for the last day that Jan Meyer was scheduled to be in Windhoek. It was to take place at a spot a great distance from the capital, but if all went well we could keep the rendezvous and still make it on to Windhoek before he had left.

We fetched the young African who was to be our guide, and set out at dawn on a track that quickly became so corrugated that we did not realize at first that something was the matter with the car itself. The crashing up and down grew more and more wild, and soon the whole front end collapsed onto the chassis. Thus pinioned, the steering apparatus was virtually useless, the shock absorbers were ruined, and everything else was in jeopardy. We fretted about Chief Kutako waiting somewhere over the horizon and Jan Meyer packing to leave Windhoek, but there was nothing to do but grind on. The racket grew worse, but our major worry was curves, and the slightest deviation on the horizon was the signal for everyone to add his hands to Sherman's on the steering wheel, to begin the battle to keep us on the road.

At last there came a contented grunt from the interpreter,

and we knew something hopeful was in sight, though what it might be we couldn't imagine. To the untrained eye there seemed only more wasted dried-out space, but presently we were told to stop the car.

"You must let me out here," he said. "It is senseless to go nearer the town together." He told us he would try to find the chief, and would return by 9:00 P.M. to fetch us at a fork four miles nearer the town. Then he said he must go quickly lest they despair of our coming, and our only link to anything vanished into the nowhere.

The route from a noted game area had crossed ours, and we went into the town as if we had just come from observing animals. There we sought help for the car, but it could not be made functional for several days at best; and Sherman left it with a man who promised to get it to Windhoek as soon as possible. We chatted among ourselves, in such a way that others would hear, about friends on a nearby farm who would be expecting us for dinner. Then we set out on foot to the fork, past anthills taller than any of us but past little else that bespoke life in the area.

It was not an easy walk, and we pondered how we would ever get to Windhoek without a car, and how we could now get the tapes and documents safely out of South West. To fly from Windhoek to Johannesburg with everything on our persons seemed to court discovery; but the only alternative was to catch Jan Meyer before he had left. So we made ourselves inconspicuous and waited impatiently until at last darkness and the Africans in an antiquated jalopy arrived almost together.

"This too does not function entirely as it should"—it was the interpreter's voice, and he was smiling at us from a front window—"but it should manage to hold together till we arrive at the place where Chief is now awaiting you. It is not too long a journey from this place to that."

The hut of our meeting was ramshackle and cold, flecked by shadows from a kerosene lamp that provided the only interruptions of the darkness. Hosea Kutako was seated at a table in the center of the hut, surrounded by nine Herero tribesmen. He wore a heavy dark greatcoat against the desert winter night, and at his right hand was a cane.

He rose as we entered, and all around him rose too. His hands swallowed and warmed ours, and we stood, reluctant to break the silence with the banalities of greeting-words, until finally the old man spoke, and his words were translated by the guide of the day's long journey: "It is good that you have come. We are grateful that friends have come to us, for it is not allowed that we go to them."

His figure and hands were too powerful to suggest eighty-nine years; and there was a great calm about him that somehow made it impossible to picture his acting imprudently or from fear. But the most remarkable thing about him was his face— a great black expanse of furrows and wrinkles set off by eyes that told much without need of translation. All at once I understood what was meant when men said that in this face could be seen the suffering of a whole people.

"It is good that you have come." What a weary odyssey those words redeemed! We spoke of how grateful we were that he had gone to such trouble that we might meet with him; and then I said our first message was the greetings we brought from Michael Scott.

"Michael Scott," the old man said, "is for some time now kept far away, despite our pleas that he be allowed to come among us. But his heart and spirit are here, and ours are with him wherever he goes. He has carried a heavy job on his shoulders, like the Son of God when He took our sins to carry on Himself. Many nights Michael Scott carried this job here, in the Locations and in the open places. He was not afraid when the police came all around, nor when he was molested by the mosquitoes and the snakes, and by the cold and the rain. Many times, like the Son of Man, he had no place to lay his head.

"Now for many years he has carried this job at U.N.O. and everywhere he can go, working always for us, never worrying that the load grows too great for his strength. Even like the Son of Man he has suffered for us, and our grateful love is to him always. We know he will do whatever can be done, and our trust is in him. This is my message to the Reverend Scott. Not mine alone, but the message of all the people."

There came to my mind at that moment the official South African description of Michael Scott as the "self-appointed spokesman of the Herero people"; and I thought: They would describe Chief Kutako as "self-appointed" too.

Then on through an evening of shadows and hushed voices the chief spoke for the tape, and was recorded first in his own language and then as translated: "I am Hosea Kutako speaking now, and I am saying this: Our country, for quite a long time, was under the African people themselves. . . ."

Soon we were into the story of the Herero people: of the War of Extermination waged by the Germans, who had wiped out four-fifths of the tribe; of the hope, born of the Allied victory in World War I, for freedom under international supervision; and of bitter disillusion under South African rule. "The dwelling place which was given to us by God has been taken away from us, and as such today we are just like animals who have nowhere to live. . . . This country is ours . . . and we suffer for it even today. We appeal to the United Nations to give us the freedom we desire. We are suffering and have been suffering for a long time. We want freedom. . . ."

Suddenly there came the sharp noise that was the signal warning us that police had entered the area. The chief's voice quickened and lowered, but he went on talking into the ma-

chine. Cameras, used tapes, and other equipment were quickly
hidden away, and translating was dispensed with: better to record as many as possible of the chief's words; someone could
put them into English later.

Then there was a second signal of some kind—unnoticed by
us, but with swift effect among the Hereros. The chief fell suddenly silent, and after that there were no words. The interpreter
signaled to another young African, and together they slipped
out into the night. The kerosene lamp was doused, and there
was no more moving about within the hut.

Presently noises began to come from outside: feet traveling
fast on gravel; a thornbush objecting to being stepped on; more
sounds of feet; then voices—first rumbling, low, uneven; then
a calling back and forth. Now there were more crunching
noises, as of perhaps a cart being wheeled away, followed by
an interlude of heavy silence.

In the hut, tension drowned the senses like a toothache and
magnified little sounds to a greatness of inexplicit menace.
Sherman pored over the tape recorder till he had extracted the
newest reels and then slipped them into a blanket that he
shoved to the darkest corner within reach. Our minds probed
round the hut, searching the blackness for ways to get out or
places to hide, but there seemed to be neither. So we sat, and
sat, and sat, and no one spoke or moved. Outside, the noises
died away and the distant desert sounds had the night to themselves again. Our thoughts turned from escape to matters that
might present themselves at any moment: what to say if the
police should appear, and how best to say it in a sentence or
two.

At last came a commotion at the doorway, and into the hut
rushed the interpreter and his companion, summoning us out
with urgent gestures. We had begun to collect our belongings
when we heard movement behind us, and turned to find the old
man rising, his huge hand held forward and up. He said some-

thing in a voice that seemed too soft to have carried to the doorway, but the interpreter nodded and closed the door.

"Chief would like you to stay a moment longer," he said. "There is something more he wishes to say to you."

"My brothers," said Hosea Kutako, "must not go in bitterness. More bitterness can bring only more hatred, and in hatred lies help for no one. Go rather in peace, for you did not come of your own will but of God's will; and tell of our sadness, for the Creator does not wish that any of His children should live as now my people must. When you have told the story of my people to your people, and to all the people across the deserts and the seas, they will come to our help, for that too is God's will."

The old man stopped, and I talked for a moment of our gratitude for his patience with us, and of our hope that we could meet again soon, next time not as hunted animals in his own country. Then a sharp noise sounded somewhere outside, and again we moved to go; and again the old hand reached up.

"I would say yet one thing more to the great chiefs at U.N.O. and to the people of your great country. My people are few; they are far away; there are so many other things, it must be easy to forget my people. What we suffer is perhaps insignificant. I would only remind those who are more fortunate that God sent His only Son to earth to die that men could live as brothers, that men would learn to share together and to love one another. If our suffering here is not important, surely it is important that so many of our brothers everywhere are weary and heavy-worn.

"It is our prayer that those who have so much will remember the sacrifice of God before it is too late. If they do not soon remember, I fear they will one day suffer as my people do, for even the patience of God can run out."

We understood at that moment the ancient impulse of men to prostrate themselves at the feet of greatness. Instead we

heard ourselves swallowing in the silence, and slipped out into
the inscrutable darkness to evade those who uphold Christian
civilization by hunting men down for speaking of brotherhood
without the proper passes. And we tried to remember that an
old man who had suffered throughout his life at the hands of
such men had told us we must love them, for they too were our
brothers.

An ancient vehicle of indeterminate make was drawn close
to the hut, and we were hastened into this contraption in a
scene of frenzied pantomime. The interpreter motioned us in
the back door and then pushed our heads down until they were
below window level. He threw us an aged and very rank horse
blanket and indicated that we should hide under it. Soon there
came a great throbbing wheeze, and the car was moving. Still
no one spoke.

The three of us in the back, adjusted slowly to the floor,
limbs scattered here and there and in one another's ribs and
eyes with each new bump. I found myself conscious of the
noise of each breath, as one is when in bed and unable to sleep.
At first we had no sense of being followed, and thoughts of
escape revived. We even wondered if the tired old jalopy might
be carrying us on to Windhoek, and in the fanciful hopefulness
of the moment half persuaded ourselves that it could make such
a journey.

Then without any warning there came a great lurch, followed
by a spasm of noisy speed and a turning so sharp it seemed
unpremeditated. I caught a streak of light somewhere behind
us, and knew again the feeling of the fugitive, the creeping
nausea of helplessness that is perhaps the worst part of concealed flight. Still we bumped along, the vehicle groaning almost as if it shared our fears and could bear them no longer.
Still no one spoke or even whispered; everyone breathed and

breathed, and the blanket smelled, and we were suddenly aware that it was very cold.

I was wondering if the lights were too close behind us to risk exposing my head to breathe some fresh air, when suddenly the wheezing and screeching stopped, and in the sudden stillness everything seemed numb. I heard the driver urging us out of the car: "Quickly. *Now!*"

The whispers sounded strange and silly against the vast dark emptiness which was all there was anywhere as we crept out and stretched and scratched and blinked, and thanked the driver, and checked to see that we had all our possessions— the tapes and film in Emory's pockets, everything else slung over shoulders and around necks. We began to talk to the driver about geography and plans; but far off, whence it seemed we had just come, there was a flickering, as of lights not quite in sight but not out of sight either. Then the car started up again with a great squeaking and gnashing of tires and gears, and the driver was hissing something at us in the midst of all the racket. The taillights fled; and we were alone, no one knew where or how far from where.

"We'll have to lie low till he gets back," I said. "But it shouldn't take too long to get rid of the other car."

"Till who gets back?" Emory asked, and we discovered we all had different notions of what the driver had said in parting. He was going to try to draw "them" off somewhere, but what after that? Was anyone coming back for us or not? Should we lie low and wait, or get as far away as possible before daybreak? Even as we first realized the implications of the confusion, the distant glimmer burgeoned into two moving headlights quickly becoming less distant. We raced away from them, crouching low against the horizons in gulleys and behind slight ridges, running away from the road and across sand punctuated by thornbushes.

But here, to men in a vehicle no less than to men on foot, a road is more a guideline than a necessity, and the car ranged back and forth across the countryside, now closing in like an aardvark on ants, now veering off to follow some shadow glimpsed elsewhere. In time the running became futile and would soon become dangerous, because the gap was too small and the gulleys and ridges were too slight to be shield enough for further movement. So we fell to the cold ground and hugged it, and tried to get our wind back as silently as possible while the vehicle drew almost parallel to us and stopped.

Sharp winds cut through tattered clothes, and our teeth made noises from the shivering. The headlights were now a spotlight aimed directly at us, and the vehicle was so near we could distinguish voices from other sounds. We dug into little holes and wondered if the police knew whom they were looking for and, if so, what they knew of our activities. None of us wanted to go to jail, but we were agreed that if we were caught we could not plead guilty—guilty of *what?* How can you plead guilty to things for which there is no guilt: for visiting people in their homes, for ignoring racial pass laws in a country that is a "Sacred Trust of Civilization"? How do you shake the hand of Hosea Kutako one minute and say you knew it was a crime the next?

And if you plead guilty to these things, how do you explain that you do this in hopes of going to freedom instead of to jail? How do you explain this and still ask the trust of those who have no such option and who have undergone so much greater risks to help you?

At length the headlights moved on perhaps five hundred feet, and there stopped again. Now two men were stomping around, playing flashlights across the emptiness and calling to each other in Afrikaans; but flashlights and stomping alike seemed puny in all the vastness of the night. Even a sneeze might go unnoticed now, and we realized it was almost impossible for us to be discovered before daylight. Whoever was in the vehicle must have reached the same conclusion at about the same time, for presently, with a flurry of starts and stops and a good deal of circling about and flashing of lights, they drove off.

We were alone again, but we had still to decide what to do next. Sooner or later the sun, so welcome and so ominous, would reappear; and if discovery did not seem imminent, escape did seem impossible. How were we to go anywhere with nothing to go in?

We must have thought about such things and argued over new strategies for two frigid hours, when once again headlights loomed in the distance. Again we retreated to whispering, and lay low against the cold sand and felt the desert thorns pricking goosepimples.

But as the lights drew nearer, we saw that they were on a truck, and it seemed to progress too erratically to be a police vehicle. Whoever was in the truck was bound to be looking for us: what else could prompt a visit to such a place in the middle of the night? The truck had been in sight now for five minutes, possibly ten, and no one breathing authority, flashlight or weapon in hand, had yet appeared.

A few seconds more and the truck, wandering to a point less than fifty yards away, had slowed almost to a stop. We sneaked across the dark toward its rear until it was clear that the vehicle needed painting and that it was falling apart behind the cab. I whispered: "If we don't try now, we're stuck till daylight. I'm going to get in as close as I can. You keep the stuff, and stay together. If I'm not back in a few minutes, stay hidden until the truck has left, no matter how long it takes."

I knew that if I waited there would be an argument about who should advance on the truck, so I moved quickly away from Sherman and Emory, leaving the tapes with them and them to their fate. Then I worked my way warily toward the lights.

I could not have gone more than a few feet when the truck started off again. I broke into a trot as it cut to its right. It seemed to pick up speed, and I ran faster, wondering if I dared to call out.

Suddenly the motor stopped and a man was out the door, and we were racing toward each other. Then we were laughing and slapping each other's backs, and gasping for air, and waving for Emory and Sherman to join us. It was the young Herero interpreter, and what a night he had had!

As soon as we had been dropped, he had set out to get help to us. He discovered that there was only one African in the area who had a motor vehicle in sufficiently good condition to have a chance of making it to Windhoek, but that African had no gasoline. There was only one African who had enough gas to get to Windhoek, but he had no vehicle. And neither of these men had a permit to be out at night. But there were two other Africans who did have such permits, although they had neither vehicle nor gas. And now, guided and fortified by the young interpreter, here were the two Africans with passes in another African's truck, operating on still another African's gasoline.

We declined seats up front, and made places for ourselves in the open part behind the cab, amidst barrels and cans and rags left from the affairs of the day. Then we rode off into the night, shivering and singing. Soon we would be in Windhoek— suddenly Shangri-La instead of a town to avoid—soon enough, with luck, to find Jan Meyer and get the accumulated tape and film out of the country.

The freezing air rolled in and seemed to carve routes through us. Soon singing seemed absurd and presently became impossible. We sought sleep, and stacked and prodded debris and groped for softness to lean against, and huddled at last into a nap; until a greater lurch than most toppled debris onto heads and knees, and sleep became a haven we could neither forget nor achieve. Shangri-La seemed farther and farther away, and hardly Shangri-La any more. Reality reasserted itself, and Windhoek was, after all, only Windhoek: we were too far off schedule to have much chance of catching Jan Meyer; if we missed him, there we would be, tapes and all, without a car, wingless birds in a den of cats.

There came the feeling that we would never be warm again, would never be done with the nightmare of flight. Then we remembered how little we had in fact gone through compared with our friends up front who had been relegated by some fate to shivering not through one night but through life, and who were engulfed in terror of police not once but always; and then we were ashamed to be cringing from fleeting and petty discomforts.

The truck bounced and joggled on and on through the great dark night, and had neither passed nor faced another light for hours when at last it heaved to a halt. We scrambled out, too cold to do more than jump around and beat our limbs together. The interpreter said that now we must trade seats, for we were only halfway to Windhoek, and the cold in the back of the truck must be frightful. But we insisted not; mostly, I think, we wanted to balance by at least one night the unequal shiverings of our different lives.

It was nearly 4:00 A.M., and the menace of dawn hastened us until it seemed impossible that the old truck would not fly apart somewhere. But the road improved as we neared the capital, and soon we began to encounter headlights; we tucked ourselves in to be sure nothing hinted of the strange cargo hurtling uncomfortably through the countryside.

We beat daylight to Windhoek, but there was no assurance that we could find Jan Meyer in the few minutes that remained before the city awakened. None of us knew much about Windhoek, and to strangers wandering about in the dark the residential areas seemed an uncharted labyrinth. Time was limited, for once people were about we could no longer endanger the Africans by crouching in their truck.

The white man's Windhoek is an improbable little town of Teutonic castles, superb modern buildings, and comfortable suburban villas. Virtually all the paved streets in the Territory are here, where sprawl some 25,000 contented Europeans. A mile or two across town an equal number of human beings— the servants and the families of the servants of the Europeans —are compressed into an area one eighty-fifth as big; but this area, the Location, is of no particular interest to those not obliged to live in it, until it becomes necessary to find more land to house white settlers.

But we were not in the Location that morning. We were in a pleasant world where everyone knows everyone else and there is no problem of finding the place where someone else lives; and where therefore street signs expire with the business district, and beyond that the outsider must stumble and guess if he cannot ask his way around.

Jan Meyer had given us a street map and a vague diagram of his house that were drawn on opposite sides of a crumbling piece of paper. The absence of street signs further reduced the usefulness of the map, which was in any case nearly illegible after a week of being folded and stuffed away. Furthermore, the route to the house was indicated from a spot that we could not locate; while the only clue yielded by a study of the diagram was the location of a night light that was to be left burning by a side door. Thus our wanderings were a bit haphazard; from our niches in the rear there seemed no limit to the number of times we could drive past some irrelevant point. Meanwhile, people and vehicles had started to appear on the streets.

At length the driver pulled the truck off into a deserted alley-

way, and we all pored over the scrap of paper. We agreed that
ten minutes was as much longer as Emory, Sherman, and I
could remain in the truck. After that we would be dropped
nearer to downtown Windhoek, and the Africans would proceed with tapes, film, and documents to the Location, where
the interpreter would conceal them for the next day or two.

Then we tried to arrange a subsequent rendezvous and a
way to get messages back and forth. Suddenly Sherman, who
had been studying the map while everyone else haggled, repressed a little cry. "It's a miracle!" he said, waving at a building outlined against the fragmentary daylight; and there, not
two blocks away, stood the elusive landmark of the starting-
point of our directions.

We followed the turns indicated on the map until we came
to the general area of the house of Jan Meyer, and then we
drove up and down, hoping to see a houselight somewhere. The
section is a lovely one, full of sharp rises and angled slopes
that offered a variety of splendid views in the advancing dawn;
but these were lost to us in the weary race to beat daylight.

We were far enough out from town now for the streets again
to be deserted, and we drove along with less caution and more
craning of necks. There were false alarms, and conflicting opinions about turns; and then, as welcome as the Pacific to Balboa,
a light—hazy in the newness of morning, but a light on the
side of a house not quite a block away. Someone said the house
didn't fit the diagram very closely. For a moment I hesitated,
and then I knew there was nothing to do but try, so I left the
old truck a block behind and walked up to the door and
knocked. For a long instant there was silence. Then I knocked
again, louder, more insistently, and suddenly the door opened;
and it was our man in Windhoek.

"Man," he said, "I thought you'd never get here! I leave for
the airport in twenty minutes, you know."

An hour later, most of what we had collected in South West

was on its way out of the Territory. There was no reason to think that the police knew yet that they had been searching for *us*, but circumstances were closing in and it would be wise to get ourselves out as quickly as possible.

I had a confirmed seat on the next plane to Johannesburg. There I would have overnight to run errands, and with a confirmed seat to Nairobi the next day, there seemed no reason why I could not be out of South Africa before my extended visa had expired.

Emory and Sherman had no difficulty getting reservations on planes that left later in the week, but when I checked in at BOAC I was informed that my flight from Windhoek to Johannesburg was overbooked. Confirmed ticket or not, there was no way to get me on.

"In that case why is my ticket plainly marked 'O.K.'?" I demanded that they telephone the Johannesburg BOAC office, a procedure that appeared to absorb the efforts of several people for several hours and finally produced the information that the girl in Johannesburg had "thought" there was a seat when she confirmed my ticket.

Why should I be bumped because BOAC was careless about issuing tickets? I threatened lawsuits and cables to London, but the nearest thing I could get to an answer was that a Rhodesian high school soccer team was to be aboard, and of course they all had to travel together.

The soccer players were resting at the Continental Hotel. There I talked my way through a succession of clerks and managers by persuading them that I was an old star bearing tips for the Rhodesian squad, but it was all in vain. The squad was determined to travel as a unit; besides, to wait for the next plane would mean being late for some function they could not miss in Salisbury.

Time was running out, and we were becoming conspicuous in a town full of pitfalls and officials. How long did we have to get out of South Africa before the police would finger the foreigners who happened to be in South West at the precise time that illicit mixed meetings were reported in remote areas?

We turned to expedients that would have been foolish in less difficult circumstances. Prominent Europeans were apprised of my difficulty—all the air connections that would be missed throughout Africa provided sufficient reason to be upset without mentioning visas—and with an energetic graciousness that discomfited us even as we prayed it would succeed, they set out to help. Airline officials were phoned, rulebooks reexamined, and strings pulled, or at least pulled at. At first we thought all the activity might stir suspicion, but everyone seemed content to believe we had been wandering around in game reserves and the like.

While all this was going on, I tracked down an officer of the plane itself. I doubt if he had ever heard a sadder tale in so remote a spot, and he promised to do whatever he could. I sat down in the lobby of the Continental and was wondering if there was anything else to try when I heard my name, and turned to find the officer of the plane. What had transpired I do not know; I did not ask. I might do a grave disservice if I said I thought he had guessed more about my plight than I had told him, and had therefore determined to help; more likely someone's string-pulling had at last reached the right spot. At any rate, I was told I would be allowed on the plane, in the seat normally reserved for the stewardess, and that all I had to do was appear on time at the airport in the morning.

Emory, Sherman, and I made plans about when and where we would get together again, and then parted with the melodramatic premonitions of Army buddies suddenly forced to swim the Yalu separately. Everything went well at the airport, and soon I was flying out of South West over sand so unbroken it seemed more a drained ocean dotted with occasional islands of human habitation than a vast and troubled land.

I thought of the things we had done, and the things we had not done, and of the things there were now to do; and then we had passed what it had taken days to drive, and were over the diamond fields at Kimberley. It seemed deranged that so much wealth and so much room were insufficient for so few people: if human beings could not figure out some way to live decent lives together with such opportunities as these, surely there could be little hope for the rest of the globe. I thought of the terrible things men were doing to each other a mile below me, despite all there was of riches and space, and of the more terrible things they would do before the will of the God of Hosea Kutako had prevailed, and there was justice at last.

To my right and left were the white Rhodesian soccer players, neat and healthy in their blazers and flushed with the joy and vigor of youth. But when I looked at them I saw Markus Kooper in the desert, and the terror in the eyes of the Herero woman with the dog; and there came again the smell of the rancid hovels where fester the scars and sores and the empty stomachs of those who draw the water and hew the wood and dig the ore without which there could be no swimming pools or tennis courts or mansions in southern Africa.

I wanted to cry for the black children in their rags and rashes who have no youth and no joy, and for the white children who cannot know what the behavior of their parents has done to the hearts of their neighbors; and for all the land that soon would have to endure the fangs of unleashed hate, would have to watch the children of this man kill the children of that. Would have to watch this while the ghosts of thousands of years of human anguish wondered at the madness of heirs who could learn so much about some things and so little about others.

But such thoughts were my own. On my left the Rhodesian soccer players were singing, *What's the use of worrying?—It never was worth while,* and on my right they were singing *Mañana,* so that the two songs came out mixed together; and if I could not blame these happy, singing young lords of the earth for their good fortune or for the misfortune of so many others, neither could I forgive them their cocky, charming indifference to these misfortunes. And if this was unfair, it was hardly as unfair as the strange caprice that gives so much to some and so little to others, depending on the amount and distribution of melanin in their skins.

There was too much to do during the last few hours in Johannesburg, but I was glad the last hours had come. All three of us were beginning to feel more hunted than followed. Enemies had begun to seem ubiquitous and friends suspect, and our perspective was becoming too corroded to judge what was possible or even what was important. We yearned to make an unguarded phone call. It seemed a distant luxury.

I knew I should not soon see Johannesburg again, and was full of last-minute things I wanted to do and places I wanted to go. I had not expected to feel this way, but so it was, even in the rush to collect tapes, films, and documents, and to make the necessary farewells and reports.

I have been in some cities that are larger and many that are more beautiful, but I have known none as challenging, none whose flavor and ghost last so long and haunt so relentlessly. There are no other cities like Johannesburg; there should be no others. One such place is too many. Yet what magic there is in this strange, teeming, undigested mixture of El Dorado and the Black Hole, of Wall Street in the '20's and Berlin in the '30's, this bush village exploded by gold and diamonds in less years than a man's life into bottomless slums and endless suburbs and all the pulsing racket of the metropolis between; exploded until it has become, without design or conscious choice, Mecca to black men seeking work and Westchester County to white women seeking play, and how much more to how many others: and to me, as no foreign place before or since, home.

Then all at once it was time to leave, and I girded myself with a lawyer, alerted a reporter, and headed for the airport. I took with me nothing that could not be replaced if confiscated, and little that was controversial. What material I did have that might incur official displeasure was buried under several layers of Nationalist propaganda.

There were two pleasant surprises at the airport. Emory arrived from Windhoek in time to join me in the exiting procedure; and nothing happened when we went through Customs. It began to seem silly to have worried about being allowed to leave; after all, why shouldn't the government do everything possible to speed us on our way? Indeed, everyone was most helpful, and we completed the formalities ten minutes before flight time and headed toward the anteroom where we were to say the last goodbyes. We never reached it.

Halfway there, we saw people pointing toward the ceiling, and looked up to discover a number of uniformed men, some with binoculars, peering down from a balcony. There was a good deal of excited gesturing, much of it in our direction. But Emory and I had just cleared Customs and Immigration, everything was in order, and there was no reason for concern.

We began to look around to see if we could spot a cause for the commotion anywhere in the crowd. A moment later the lawyer and a friend brushed by. "You're being followed. Careful!" he mumbled, and vanished. Then everything happened at once.

The BOAC hostess called our flight, and passengers were asked to start boarding. Three uniformed men surrounded Emory, and I was taken in tow by several others. Elderly ladies gasped, necks craned, and everyone pushed and whispered. The whole thing seemed too Hollywood to be happening—but here were the police, there was the plane, and no way out suggested itself.

The police began ferreting piece by piece through what little we had in the way of belongings. For some reason the top layer of Afrikaans propaganda seemed to enthrall them. They pored over each booklet, fingered between the pages, and finally one who seemed to be in charge demanded what we were doing with "all these books."

I said in a surprised tone that many South Africans had told us they felt they were misunderstood abroad, and we were taking along material to help explain all points of view. This caused a lot of whispering and nodding, but nothing more was said about the printed matter. Attention wandered to the unrewarding remnants of unwashed underclothes and crumbling travel brochures.

The stewardess gave the last call for boarding. I stared at the stream of passengers walking through the doorway to the ramp; and still the ransacking went on. Soon all the other passengers had boarded the plane, and I suddenly thought: *They're doing this to make us miss the plane so they can play with us as long as they want to.* It came to me that they must be on very uncertain ground to try to keep us from leaving in such a clumsy way, and that it made no sense to stand by meekly. "Come on," I said in a voice pitched as loud as I could manage short of a bellow, "you've been through everything two or three times, and we're going to miss our plane!"

My protesting grew vehement and began to arouse interest around the terminal. I decided to address my remarks to the expanding knot of the curious standing all around us: "What kind of country is this? We go through all your official red tape, and then, as our flight is taking off, this happens."

I had just announced a crusade to tell every American about the mistreatment they would be subjected to if they ever set foot in the Union when we saw our friends elbow in from the fringe of the crowd. They nodded, and I knew the reporter was due at any minute.

My tirade was attracting more and more people, and the official who seemed to be in charge of the searching party told me to calm down. A number of voices in the crowd expressed sympathy or indignation, and some offered earnest advice in Afrikaans to the officials, who seemed to be growing confused. I thought: *If that plane will just wait a minute more, we'll be on it.*

The airline hostess appeared in the distance, and I shouted to her: "What do these men want? They're going to make us miss the plane!" She made her way quickly to our side and in a moment had taken over the battle to get us loose.

She asked what the trouble was, and, receiving no clear reply, proceeded to berate functionaries who delay dozens of passengers to make themselves feel important. Her outrage turned the trick. Not a word was said to us, but before we knew what had happened the police had evaporated and we were racing through the crowd to the plane.

There was a coda to the getting out.

Sherman was the last to leave, and did not get to Jan Smuts until midmorning several days after we had gone. By then he was sleepless, overwrought, and expecting the worst, as his diary testifies: "Special Branch isn't waiting, thank God!" is the comment dated July 31st at 10:45 A.M., just after his plane had landed in Johannesburg. He searched in vain for the person who was supposed to meet him with a ticket for the 12:45

P.M. flight to Nairobi, and to whom, before going through Customs, he was to deliver the last batch of materials collected in South West.

Eleven-thirty came and went, then noon, then a quarter after. Sherman alternated between prowling around the airport searching for his contact and hiding from people who had uniforms on or whom he thought looked suspicious. At 12:17 he was hiding, and scribbled in the diary, "I'm sunk!"

Finally he stuffed notes and rolls of film in his shoes and into rolled-up pairs of socks, crumpled the diary until it fitted into the part of his flashlight that normally houses batteries, and plunged into the Customs procedures. If all went well, and if some miracle should bring his ticket at the last moment, he could still make the plane. The next entry in the diary, made considerably later, describes what followed: "I stride up terrified but look enthusiastic, like a touring white hunter. They say I'm late for the plane and never even ask a question! Now all I needed was a ticket!"

There remained twelve minutes until flight time. According to the diary, he had cursed and prayed for six of these when all at once a car came screaming up to the terminal: "My savior—drove nineteen miles in fifteen minutes with the ticket, and is shaking like a leaf—but I had a *ticket!*"

Then came a dash through the gate to the ramp. Waiting there, as in any first-class nightmare, was "a pack of cops." At this point reflexes took over; and Sherman, breathless, and "fully expecting to be pinched," raced past the uniforms onto the plane, ran the length of the aisle, and collapsed panting into an empty seat.

Before he had time to catch his breath, a soft feminine voice with an English accent came from the neighboring place: "There, there," it said, "take it easy—you're on British territory now. Everything will be all right."

And so it was.

VIII Not many private citizens of the United States have had occasion to speak before a committee of the General Assembly of the United Nations, and we approached the event with some trepidation.

Our observations and the material we had collected would be germane to the work of the Committee on South West Africa and to the work of its parent body, the Fourth Committee of the General Assembly, which deals with matters involving trusteeship and non-self-governing territories.

The Committee on South West Africa submits its annual report to the Fourth Committee, and it is here that U.N. policies on South West are hammered out. Recommendations of the Fourth Committee are not ordinarily rejected by the General Assembly, inasmuch as every nation represented in the General Assembly is represented on the Fourth Committee as well.

We would have to request permission to testify before these groups, but the advisory opinion of the World Court and the precedents of the past several General Assemblies would support our petitions. Beyond that, our position was in some ways an ambiguous one. We had originally planned to speak as individuals, but many Africans in South West asked us to join Michael Scott, Kerina, and Kozonguizi in representing them at the United Nations, or simply assumed we would do so.

Furthermore, whatever our technical status, we were still Americans, and did not wish to do anything that might embarrass our own government.

But both conflicts came to seem more theoretical than actual. What we wanted to say was not at variance with what the South West Africans wanted us to say; and it was hard to see how Americans appearing as spokesmen for the rights of Africans in an international territory could embarrass the United States at the U.N.

In fact, the situation could hardly have been a better one for the American Delegation. It could vote in favor of our applications on the narrowest legal grounds, enjoy the benefits of our being Americans if we did well, and disclaim us if we performed irresponsibly.

Our uncertainty about whether to petition as individuals or as spokesmen for Africans was resolved by two cables which arrived as if by telepathy. Both were from Chief Kutako, Chief Witbooi, and Sam Nuyoma, President of the Ovamboland People's Organization (now the South West Africa People's Organization); one was addressed to me and one to the United Nations. The intention of the cables was merely to "authorize" us to appear as spokesmen, but there was something about them—some tone of trust, almost as if we had become a part of the peoples represented in the signature—that made it seem unthinkable to appear in any other way.

I paid an early visit to the United States Mission, where a pleasant official assured me the odds were "99 to 1" that the United States would vote to hear us. I assumed the "1" was a precaution lest a check turn up evidence that we were in some way not loyal Americans, and offered to bring references or any information that might facilitate such a check. I was told this would not be necessary. If any question arose about the position of the United States, I would be notified. There the matter rested until the day before the Fourth Committee was to vote.

By that time Eric Louw, the Foreign Minister of South Africa, had attacked Emory, Sherman, and me in an angry harangue that was imprecise but included a pointed threat to the United States Government. Mr. Louw's chief contention appeared to be that we were sinister figures discredited at home and subsidized by some vast international network of spies and subversives. It did not seem inappropriate to hope that the United States Delegation might offer to correct some of the more flamboyant misrepresentations, but late on the afternoon before the vote I chanced upon the congressman who was the temporary American representative on the Fourth Committee and learned instead that the United States had decided to abstain.

My indignation puzzled the congressman: such an abstention would not affect our being heard, since we would win by a large majority in any case. The United States had to abstain, he explained, to avoid jeopardizing visas for Americans who might wish to go to South Africa. It would be a different story if it were the internal affairs of our own country that we wanted to speak about—he would always support the right of Americans to do that; it was this business of speaking for foreigners that he couldn't see.

I wondered if someone so unburdened by knowledge about U.N. rules and United States policies might not also be misinformed about how the delegation was going to vote on what was, after all, only a minor procedural matter. The prospect of being heard with the support of the Afro-Asians, most of the Latins, and the Soviet bloc, but not that of the United States, was distressing and absurd. The petitions of Americans concerned about colonialism and racial oppression would thus be transformed into evidence of the official indifference of their government, and this roll call could become another item of communist propaganda.

We decided to pursue the matter further, and in the few hours that remained before the vote spoke to as many officials of the United States Mission as we could reach. We heard no more about the imperiled visas or the right of Americans to tell their domestic grievances at the U.N., but there was a full supply of new excuses hardly less novel. Of these my favorite was the one offered by a man whose job was, I believe, in public relations. He said it was better that the United States not vote for our applications because American support might be awkward for *us*.

One official told me that our testifying might create "a precedent," and "hordes" of "less responsible" Americans might embarrass the United States Government by asking to appear. The possibility of future irresponsible applications seemed a rather odd excuse for not supporting current responsible ones, but the official grew irate when I protested, and informed me in some heat that how the United States voted was none of my business. "We make such decisions," he announced, "and you have a hell of a nerve butting in." I asked if it was his view that how their delegation voted at the U.N. was none of the business of the American people in general, and he retreated: the United States could not vote for us because it "could not afford" to let it seem that it might have "sponsored" us.

Our experience was more symptomatic than significant. Similar procedural evasions, and inconsistent or indifferent attitudes in the lobbies, have often hurt the United States through the years. And we were to discover that the way a nation— especially a great power—used its weight in the constant off-stage maneuverings is taken as a more enduring test of its attitude than an occasional much-trumpeted vote on some major issue. Indeed, a delegation that ultimately votes for a

resolution it has tried to emasculate or lobby to death may find
its reward in heightened distrust of its motives.

Furthermore, on such deeply emotional issues as racial oppression there is no substitute for energetic and passionate involvement by individual delegates. The efforts of Mason Sears,
for many years the Permanent American Representative to the
Trusteeship Council, were a greater asset to his country than
countless mechanical assurances of sympathy by diplomats too
pressed or too lofty to try to understand the moods and points
of view of delegates of other races and continents. And Senator
Wayne Morse won the admiration and gratitude of a wide cross
section of U.N. delegates with his remarkably fine work in the
Fourth Committee. Indeed the American people are most fortunate that there have always been some dedicated people on the
staff of the United States Mission, as well as some transient
members of American delegations to the General Assembly,
whose personal efforts have helped ease the consequences of the
fumblings of their government.

The voting on the petitions was without surprise. Thirteen
requests had been received by the Fourth Committee, and all
were granted, but the policy of the South African Government
and the cost of traveling to New York prevented six of the
petitioners from appearing in person. Kozonguizi was already
in New York, but it was not certain that Hans Beukes would
have enough money to arrive in time until at the last moment
the delegates to the annual Congress of the United States National Student Association contributed $800 for his air fare.

Thus, in the end, five new petitioners plus Michael Scott and
Mburumba Kerina were to testify. Emory, Sherman, and I
tried to divide our material to minimize repetition. Father
Scott, Kerina, Kozonguizi, and Beukes did not see our testimony in advance, let alone seek to influence it in any way.

The seven of us did confer about the sequence in which we

should make our statements, and about the steps we would urge the U.N. to take in South West Africa. The further re-iteration of resolutions adopted and ignored through the years seemed inadequate. A number of fresh approaches had been proposed, but the most promising seemed to be the suggestion, first made by India several years earlier, that the compulsory jurisdiction of the International Court of Justice be invoked.

The Court's three advisory opinions about South West were not legally binding, and had been disregarded by South Africa. But under the terms of Article 7 of the Mandate Treaty a state that has been a member of the League of Nations (and possibly certain others as well) can require the Mandatory Power to defend its stewardship before the Court. Should it refuse to do so, the Court may conduct *ex parte* proceedings anyway. With overwhelming evidence of South Africa's viola-tions of her Mandate now available, the Court might order the Union Government to abandon her race policies in South West or to abandon the Territory itself. A Court ruling after litigation under Article 7 would be binding on the parties involved, and defiance could incur sanctions or such other measures as the Security Council or General Assembly might deem necessary.

Of the African members of the U.N., at least Liberia and Ethiopia were qualified to initiate such a suit. There was reason to believe they would agree to do so in conjunction with a U.N. resolution referring favorably to the possibility of this kind of action, and we agreed to press for such a resolution.

The matter of the tape recordings was still in abeyance. We decided to ask permission to play excerpts for the committee at the end of our opening remarks, although there was no clear precedent for this. Nevertheless the tapes had now to be pre-pared, and this proved to be a most complicated operation. The recordings had to be transposed onto a machine that could be heard over the U.N. earphones. Clear translations had to be dubbed in where the originals were blurred or inadequate; and some order had to be introduced into the jumbled tangle of tribal and European words. All this would have been impossible without the help of a young Episcopal seminarian named Fred Boynton, who sat imperturbably manipulating three or four gadgets night after night until an audible and coherent progression emerged.

On October 13, 1959, the Honorable N. Pilar of Indonesia, Chairman of the Fourth Committee, invited us to take seats at tables in the center of the great hall where the Fourth Committee meets.

All at once History was not somewhere else. My thoughts kept straying to wretched, underfed people in crumbling shacks praying for help so they could begin life, and sometimes it was hard not to resent statesmen in air-conditioned comfort playing chess with their miseries. It seemed gross that ineptness on my part might mute cries so stark that everyone should be able to hear them without intermediaries.

Fortunately, mine was a small part of the presentation. Mburumba Kerina gave a striking résumé of South Africa's violations of legal obligations, and Kozonguizi submitted a mass of detail about the daily life of non-Europeans that accumulated into one of the most impressive indictments of the policies of the Union Government ever offered at the United Nations. Hans Beukes's testimony provided the committee with its first first-person information about the position of the Coloured population of South West, and his personal story stirred more interest than it might otherwise have because Eric Louw had attacked him in a peculiarly vindictive way.

As a matter of fact, as time went on we came to feel a reluctant gratitude to Eric Louw. He flailed away at a list of villains that seemed endless. The Committee on South West

Africa headed the list, but at one time or another he managed
to find something sinister about such diverse entities as the
representative union of students of his own country and a
highly respected American organization which he had praised
in Parliament only a few weeks earlier. Even Sweden was not
immune: what impertinence for Swedes to criticize South Africa's race policies in view of their own treatment of the Lapps!
Much of what he said specifically about us was patent nonsense, and the process of refuting it added to our credibility
when there arose other differences about facts more difficult
to check.

Two of Mr. Louw's more striking lapses seemed particularly
foolish. In his zeal to challenge Hans's *bona fides* as a representative of Rehoboth, he read from newspaper articles that
included a repudiation of Hans by his family and other community leaders. The accuracy of the quotes was vouched for by
a government official who swore they were uttered in his
presence. These statements made before a government official
provided an interesting contrast with statements contained in
letters Hans had received from the same people; it was not
easy to miss the implication of intimidation. But more astonishing was the discovery that Mr. Louw had abandoned reading
one of the articles halfway through, and in such a way as to
convey an opposite impression from that conveyed by a reading
of the whole article.

Then he made what he must have felt the Fourth Committee
would view as a very serious indictment of Emory, Sherman,
and me. We had, he said, procured our visas to go to South
West Africa by fraud. Quite apart from the fact that few people
other than South African Government officials would have considered such a deed censorious if true, it happened not to be
true. As Emory put it:

"Stating repeatedly that his speech was a presentation of

facts, Mr. Louw had these things to say about me: that I first
visited South Africa two or three years ago on a student tour;
that I was subsidized on this summer's trip by certain American
organizations; and that I falsified my visa application by applying as a student going to South Africa to study flora and fauna.
Gentlemen, all of these statements—and others—are completely false. Not only are they not facts—they are not even
misrepresentations of facts; they are utter falsehoods.

"I certainly admit . . . that I was not prepared to point
out to the South African Government that I wished to travel
to South West Africa in order to gain an independent evalua-
tion of the state of the people in that territory. Because had I
done so, I believe that the South African administration would
have done what it could to prevent such independent observa-
tion."

The Chairman of the Fourth Committee suggested that
Emory substitute a less unparliamentary term for the word
"falsehood," but the mood of the committee may be inferred
from the fact that after a flurry of discussion the word was
allowed to stand. Subsequently, as if to corroborate at least
one of the specific charges, Mr. Louw's deputy read from the
visa applications, which turned out to contain no reference to
"flora and fauna" after all. The reference to "flora and fauna,"
he then explained, was contained in "private papers which have
come into the possession of the South African Government"—
whereupon the Fourth Committee was read excerpts from one
of the carbons that had been in the luggage purloined from our
car in Johannesburg!

Such a silly performance did little to increase faith in the
general reliability of pronouncements of the South African
Government. One delegate even remarked that "the statements
of the distinguished Minister of External Affairs of the Union

of South Africa seem to have been a vast reservoir of inexactitudes."

Several delegates came to our defense. A number of complimentary letters from prominent Americans were read into the record, and when Mr. Louw proceeded to walk out before we could reply to his allegations, he left behind an atmosphere substantially more sympathetic to us than it might otherwise have been. South Africa always stages a ceremonial walkout after attacking the petitioners and then sits in the gallery while they are discussing South West Africa, apparently indifferent to the boon this ritual provides for her critics. At one point during the Fourteenth Session an indignant delegate of considerable eminence roared at South Africa's empty seat, "I am not accustomed to debating with ghosts!"

But all in all I think the younger petitioners themselves were the most effective refutations of Eric Louw. Four of them— Kozo, Sherman, Emory, and Hans—were new figures to the members of the Fourth Committee. It is hard to judge such things when one is a participant, but I found among reporters and observers no dissent from my feeling that their dignity and simplicity, unconscious and unfailing through the most trying moments, bespoke an integrity impervious to sniping.

Emory's and Sherman's prepared statements were brief. Emory's began:

"I cannot express how much it means to me to have the privilege of appearing before you and of being able to testify about the things that I have observed in the Territory of South West Africa. I am going to comment only briefly because Mr. Bull, Mr. Lowenstein, and I have composed our thoughts in greater detail in a testimony that will be delivered by Mr. Lowenstein."

Then, after discussing the South African accusations, he gave his impressions of the conditions under which non-Europeans live in South West:

"In a nutshell, they possess virtually none of the freedoms that are the God-given right of all human beings. . . . They have no vote and no representation. They are relegated to inferior, low-paying jobs. They cannot be absent from work without permission from their employers, even when they are ill. Those in urban areas must live on government land under the most squalid conditions. Most of them can afford to eat only once a day. They cannot purchase milk except in seasons when the white population has a surplus. You can imagine what the combination of these factors—insufficient nutrition and unsanitary conditions—does to their health.

"They live in terror of the government in particular and of the white man in general. They are constantly harassed by police, and cannot voice their objections even verbally for fear of reprisal. This, by the way, is the fallacy of speaking to people in the presence of government officials.

"The African people of South West Africa are wonderful people. We share a spiritual tie inasmuch as many of them are followers of Christ, as I am. After forty years these people know that South Africa will never agree to grant them what they desire and what is rightly theirs. They have placed their faith in the United Nations in the belief that as soon as the members of this great Organization realize their plight they will be given the rights and freedoms they deserve."

Sherman's remarks followed a similar pattern. His testimony included a description of hospital arrangements in Windhoek:

"The natives' hospital consisted of a number of small, low buildings each of which was in a decrepit state. There were 250 beds and three full-time white doctors to care for the

20,000 to 30,000 non-Europeans who inhabit the Windhoek area. These doctors also had to care for the outpatients who appeared each day for treatment, usually numbering about a hundred. There are no laboratory facilities at the hospital on which to base diagnostic and therapeutic procedures. There was only one relatively primitive operating room as far as I could determine.

"The wards were overcrowded and dirty. The sanitation facilities were foul, and I can use no other word but 'foul.' There was one toilet at the end of each ward, a number of which wards I saw. These toilets were evidently clogged, for they were filled to the brim with excreted material. The mental patients were crowded into a separate ward, with no one adequately trained to care for them. There was an area set aside for the inordinately large number of tubercular patients.

"Of this last group, the tubercular patients, a member of the staff told me that at this and many native hospitals the patients find conditions so intolerable that they leave at the earliest opportunity. Several Africans told me that a common grievance is the unpalatable nature of the food, and heaven knows that the Africans are accustomed to a frugal repast. Of course, in the case of persons carrying an infectious disease such as tuberculosis, this early leaving of confinement is especially serious, for they are likely to contaminate their dwelling and working places as well as infect those people with whom they come in contact.

"The European hospital, on the other hand, was as resplendent as the native hospital was shocking. The superintendent with whom I spoke said that his only complaint about the new hospital was that it was too much like a country club. The patients' rooms were beautiful, the maximum number of patients being four per room. Each bed had a place in which to plug a telephone. There were a number of well-appointed operating rooms and laboratories. The nurses' quarters were particularly attractive, and included a swimming pool for their after-hours relaxation.

"The discrepancies between these two facilities are so obvious that although a new native hospital has been proposed, I can't help wondering why luxury should be given precedence over such dire necessity."

He concluded with "a few of the more burning images that were left with me in South West Africa:

"The first aspect of South West Africa that struck me was the acute fear that prevailed among the inhabitants of the country; and this fear was not restricted to the indigenous population but extended into the European minority as well. Among those people who would openly express their grievances to us, it was necessary to assure the majority that their names would never be mentioned in connection with what they had told us. We even talked to some Europeans of wealth and stature who made a frank discussion of politics contingent on this point.

"This is an eye-opening experience for one brought up in the democratic tradition of freedom of expression as I know it as an American.

"But a much more fundamental fear exists for ordinary folk. It is a fear that comes from living in an atmosphere . . . of complete disregard for them as individual human beings. Non-Europeans are seen more as a commodity, as units of labor, to be exploited for this purpose but to have no other function. They are never consulted about their fate. . . .

"I am not a student of politics; and while I can sympathize in the abstract sense with a people who are governed in flagrant violation of an international trust, I am no judge of legalities.

But, as a fellow human being, I cannot see how any people can be expected to live in their own country in a state where they are denied the most fundamental human rights. . . . That they can still hope is a miracle."

I too began by expressing gratitude "to those nations that voted to hear us," and talked a bit about the nature of our trip—why we had asked to testify, and what our qualifications were to do so:

"We regret that the pass laws of the Union Government, enforced—illegally, we believe—in South West Africa, made it necessary for us to meet with people of other races in places other than public halls or even private homes. But these conditions, deplorable as they are, can hardly be blamed on us, or for that matter on the non-European population of South West Africa. Nor can men of good will be expected to respect forever such monstrosities, least of all in international territory. . . .

"We are not in any sense experts on South West Africa. We are at best inadequate substitutes for the people who are experts, and who should be here speaking for themselves with a knowledge and eloquence we cannot approach. Indeed, it seems to us a most serious indictment of the attitude of the Union Government that we have to appear here at all. Clearly there would be no need to impugn the motives or besmirch the good names of any of the present petitioners if the Union Government were willing to allow the people who should be here to come.

"And I would think that it would be far better, even from the point of view of the Union Government itself, to respect the right of its South West African wards to travel abroad than to be condemned by its own repressive legislation, and then to have the words of these wards heard here anyway."

Then, after trying to summarize our observations about South West, I entered into the plea Emory, Sherman, and I had agreed should conclude our opening statements:

"It is hard to find any evidence that, despite the clear injunction of the Mandate, the Mandatory Power has done anything significant in thirty-nine years to help the indigenous population of South West Africa to develop toward self-government or to improve its living conditions; or even that it has any intentions of ever doing so. . . .

"The world is only now recovering from the war that gave birth to this Organization. That war was necessary to stop racism gone imperialist from making slaves of most human beings. But it was also fought, with its hideous toll in lives and resources and time, to make possible better things than had gone before; to make possible a world, in the words of a great American President, free from fear and want, a world in which people would be free to speak and think as conscience might dictate. . . .

"I know as do you that suffering is still the rule for the human race, and that the miseries of centuries are not eradicated in minutes. But that not everything can be done at once gives no sanction to doing nothing at all, or indeed to doing anything less than everything that can possibly be done. And surely there are some situations that cry out more cogently and with greater urgency than others.

"May I ask that you suppose for a moment that this Organization were to receive appeals for help from people who claimed to be denied the most elementary of rights because of their race; who claimed to be living in abject and enforced poverty while neighbors of another race lived in almost unequaled prosperity; who claimed that their ancestral properties were being taken from them and that their right to move about in their own land and abroad was restricted almost to the point of nonexistence. Suppose it were further alleged that by law the government over these people were selected by 10 per cent of the population, determined by race; that no voice in the determination of public policies was accorded to the remaining 90 per cent, solely because of their race. Now imagine that the ruling authority admitted—perhaps 'boasted of' would be more accurate—the existence of the laws upon which these conditions were based, and vowed that they would *never* be changed.

"Finally, conceive for a moment, if you can, that the territory ruled by this racially 'pure' 10 per cent government were an international ward, a 'Sacred Trust of Civilization,' an area not by the most generous of definitions part of anyone's 'internal affairs.'

"Here surely would seem one instance where all mankind would work together to demonstrate that, whatever disagreements may mar brotherhood or even jeopardize survival elsewhere, organized, governmentally instituted racism has no place on this planet in our time. And surely it would be intolerable that legalized racial oppression should be the avowed policy of a government holding sway over other human beings as the trustee of mankind.

"Yet these are precisely the facts of the South West African situation, and to date the great world outside this unhappy international territory has done almost nothing about it. The existence of the racially oppressive policies in South West Africa is not, in the main, even in dispute. Does anyone dispute that no non-European can vote, or that this decitizenizing is racial in origin? Does anyone pretend that equal educational or medical facilities—even if separated—are available to non-Europeans? Will someone tell us that the pass laws are the fabrication of some public relations genius seeking to discredit the South African Government by inventing diabolical rumors about regulations that simply do not exist? Or does the government in power at least seek to offer hope of something better to come?

"Quite the contrary!

". . . The apparatus of growing oppression is there for all to see, is in fact vaunted as a 'solution' to the 'native problem,' is defined and proclaimed as 'good' for the hapless folk who have nothing to say about its construction or implementation but who cannot, even by brilliance or saintliness, escape its consequences. . . . Alone and in their agony, these almost forgotten people still dare to hope that a mankind that could rise up to crush Hitler, and could unite to assert the existence of universal human rights, will not forever sit by and watch its particular wards crushed in the very name of civilization because of nothing in this world but their birth to non-European parents.

"It is these facts and these hopes that suggest that the appeals of the people of South West Africa must touch our consciences with unique urgency, even in a world torn by injustices and still so largely ruled by suffering. . . . The simple unavoidable fact is that a sacred trust of all of us now rests in the hands of the only government on earth that dares to exalt the same types of laws that were supposed to have perished with Hitler and that have been repudiated alike by science and by all religions, by the spokesmen of democracy, of communism, and of all gradations and styles of government between.

"For these and many more reasons, we have concluded that the Government of South Africa is unfit to continue as the Trustee for the conscience of civilization. . . . It is an ironic challenge and opportunity that the one government in the world based on racial discrimination should also be the one government in defiance of the United Nations, and of opinions of the International Court, about its responsibilities in an international territory. And, as recent witnesses in this troubled land, we implore the statesmen of the world, for the sake of all who crave peace and justice anywhere as well as that of the people of South West Africa, to work together here to end oppression there. For the experience gained by such cooperation in this instance could have value as example, and even as catalyst, in producing further cooperation in more complex and less clear-cut situations elsewhere. . . .

"We urge that steps be taken this year to carry the problem of the status of South West Africa to the International Court of Justice for determination under its compulsory jurisdiction. . . . In the troubled scales of the human travail, few situations have called more poignantly for action, and few situations have required less action to produce hope for results."

Michael Scott concluded the formal presentation of the petitioners, and the rasping crossfire of the days before drifted away in the unruffled progress of his words. The earphones magnified the sound of his unhurried turning of pages, and for some reason brought sharply to mind the first time I had heard him speak almost exactly one year earlier.

I pondered the strange course of events that had moved me in a year from the gallery to the petitioners' tables. Then I thought about my moments of pique with the processes of this Organization that could seem more mastodon than human, so enormous, so oblivious, so obsolescent, so slow-moving. And somehow the moments of pique seemed only footnotes to the wonder that such an Organization managed to exist at all, an Organization where statesmen from a hundred nations sit for days listening to pleas from the weakest and most remote of peoples. I found myself rejoicing that such an Organization had survived all the cynical misuse of its machinery and all the tragic moments of its failures, and that obscure and oppressed peoples still hoped in it. I understood better then the great patience-impatience of Michael Scott; and I thought about the men sitting all around us, invisible behind nameplates and expressionless faces, and prayed that somehow they could be roused to act before the great Organization had defaulted itself into impotence and men were left with the sour despair that is the hangover of frustrated hopes.

After an amiable discussion of procedural matters, the Fourth Committee decided to transcribe the tape recordings and circulate them as official documents. In addition, the tapes were to be played for any members of the committee who wished to hear them, but not at a formal sitting of the committee.

The Security Council Chamber was selected for the session with the tapes, and perhaps two-thirds of the members of the committee turned up. Sherman told a little about how the recordings had been made, and then the voices of Hosea Kutako, Samuel Witbooi, Markus Kooper, and other men so long prevented from appearing in person were at last heard at the United Nations: "I am very glad today that I know that our sorrows will be told to the people at the United Nations through the means of this machine. So I ask with all my heart that those great nations who are gathered there will help us quickly, so that we will be released even this year from the bondage of the Union of South Africa. That is the only way that we will have rights in our own country. . . ."

There were delegates jaded from too many sessions in international tugs-of-war who told us afterward that few things had stirred them as unexpectedly or as profoundly as the words of these people who had risked so much to broadcast their faith in conscience as a force in the affairs of men.

One veteran diplomat caught me by the arm as we left the chamber: "I don't know what I can do for your friends," he said, waving at the tape recorder, "but what they have done for me is remarkable. I feel I'm back at the beginning—in Lake Success or even San Francisco—and somehow it seems again that with this Organization maybe the good things are possible after all. It's extraordinary what hearing that old man did to me."

"That old man" of course was Hosea Kutako. We had forgotten the last words he had put onto the tape—the words that had had to be translated in New York because of the signal announcing the approach of the police—until they sounded through the earphones: "We want the United Nations to help us; we want them to free us. . . . It is now being said that while I have been petitioning the United Nations for such a long time . . . the United Nations has not helped me up to now and it is very unlikely that it will ever help me. That is what is being said. But I always say, and I shall always say, that I shall not stop petitioning the United Nations. This is what I had to say."

The six meetings of the committee that followed the completion of the petitioners' statements were devoted to the asking of questions. Most delegates participated, and an exhaustive range was covered.

Sometimes it was difficult to know how best to handle an inquiry. It is not always easy to gauge moods through earphones and translations, and on occasion I found myself wondering if I were talking too long or too often, or if I had missed an important nuance in some query whose point escaped me. But in general the questioning, though detailed and intense, was friendly, and the interest displayed seemed genuine and was in any case heartening. We let ourselves hope that all this interest—all these questions—must mean something would be *done* this year.

The South African Foreign Minister had announced triumphantly that our letters asking for financial assistance ("which have come into the possession of the South African Government") were "irrefutable proof" that we were "agents" of a "vast network."

No one appeared to be very alarmed by this notion of the Union Government that it was the object of a great international conspiracy. One delegate noted that "Messrs. Lowenstein, Bull, and Bundy have been accused of complicity in a vast plot," but added that "they have ably defended themselves" against the charge. Another delegate asked in a slightly bewildered tone if the petitioners would give their "views" about the South African allegation that they were "part of a plot against the Government of the Union of South Africa, to which the representative of that government has referred several times." Michael Scott replied that the Government of South Africa seemed to be "obsessed" with the idea of a plot, and went on to list a variety of groups and individuals, ranging from the International Olympic Committee to Yehudi Menuhin, who he said had protested South Africa's race policies without any need for a "plot."

"We had indeed hoped to obtain financial assistance for the trip, but unfortunately had very little luck along those lines," I said, and added that the fact that we had had to raise our own funds might more reasonably be regarded as proof that we had *not* been the "agents" of anyone. I suggested that Mr. Louw would do well to hire new secret police if the reports of his current crop really had led him to such hallucinations.

This discussion did focus attention on a question that had already aroused some curiosity, especially among nonwhite delegates, many of whom wondered what had in fact interested three white Americans in a situation so far from home, especially as racial injustices are not altogether unknown in their own country. We knew from corridor comments that some delegates suspected us—or wished others to suspect us—of being indifferent to, or even eager to divert attention from, America's shortcomings.

Toward the end of the questioning an occasion presented itself to discuss this matter. I cited a number of our earlier protests against discriminatory practices, including such things as Emory's resignation from his college fraternity, and then discussed the general question of our motivation in undertaking the trip. The official summary record of my statement reads as follows:

"Mr. Lowenstein went on to say that he and his friends had gone to South West Africa because they had felt they might be able to be of service to the truth and to human beings who, because of the accident of their birth, had been subjected to misfortune. He had spent a considerable portion of his life in the southern United States and thus was well acquainted with racial problems in his own country. He had worked against racial discrimination wherever he had been for many years. He would never forget how dreadful could be the consequences of inflaming race hatreds among even the finest of people, for he had lived through the election campaign in which Mr. Frank Graham, whom he considered to be one of the greatest human spirits in the world, had been defeated because of his refusal to swerve from his belief that men of all races were equal in the eyes of God, and should be so in the eyes of the law. Mr. Lowenstein was glad that, despite its great problems, his country was fast moving toward the time when all men would be brothers in the hearts of the people, as well as equal in the eyes of the law.

"When he had visited South Africa a year previously, he had felt there was much the rest of the world should know about the conditions imposed on human beings because of their race. In speaking to the Fourth Committee, he had not touched on the situation in the Union, since he was aware that that was outside the committee's terms of reference. He and his friends were telling of conditions in South West Africa not out of any desire to meddle in the affairs of another country, but because they were against oppression or unfair treatment of human beings anywhere in the world, and because such treatment in an international territory was the legitimate concern of the world, legally as well as morally."

When each delegation had had the opportunity to put all the questions it wished, the seven of us withdrew from the center tables to listen to the general debate from the galleries. Many delegates made generous comments about the petitioners, but a private remark made to Sherman, Emory, and me touched us beyond all the rest. One of the most illustrious members of the Fourth Committee, a gentleman who represents a nation not notably pro-Western in its sympathies, called to us one day as the auditorium was emptying.

"May I have a word with you?" he asked; and as we walked away with him I wondered what protocol we had breached. "I just wanted to tell you," he said softly, "that this has been a wonderful thing."

I began to say that anything that helped the people of South West Africa would be wonderful, but he interrupted.

"No, no, you misunderstand me," he said. "I mean that this has been a wonderful thing for *your* country."

With the withdrawal of the petitioners to the gallery, South Africa returned to the floor, although not, alas, in the person of the invaluable Eric Louw, who had left New York by this time. Attention turned to the annual report of the Committee on South West Africa, and to the various courses of action the U.N. might follow. The committee report provided a detailed analysis of the situation in the Territory, and concluded: "The Union of South Africa continues to fail to carry out the obligations it undertook to promote to the utmost the material and moral well-being and the social progress of the inhabitants of the territory." The extension of apartheid, it declared, is "a flagrant violation of the sacred trust which permeates the Mandate and the Charter of the United Nations and the Universal Declaration of Human Rights."

There were some magnificent speeches during the general debate—most notably, perhaps, those of Professor Enrique Rodríguez Fabregat of Uruguay and of Mr. Eamon Kennedy of Ireland, who were respectively Chairman and Rapporteur of the Committee on South West Africa. At first it seemed there was little more we could do, so we sat back to enjoy what became a documented rout of South Africa's position.

We soon learned, however, that work was just beginning, for the disposition of matters that are of less than primary concern is largely determined at the U.N. by the intensity and effectiveness of lobbying. In view of the necessary preoccupation with great issues, it is easy to see why this should happen, but it does put a premium on the man who knows what is most likely to sway which delegate; for in addition to subjects of general priority each delegation has topics of special interest to itself, and the temptation to logroll on items it cares less about can become at times almost irresistible.

On these lesser questions delegates often have considerable leeway to act as they deem best for their own country. In such situations the active support of a major power, or of a group of states whose votes may in turn be needed on some other issue, is almost indispensable if much progress is to be made,

although selfless persistence like Michael Scott's has moved
mountains over the years. Public testimony and debates about
little-known situations are useful in the effort to arouse public
opinion, but it is difficult to make public opinion a significant
force when there is not much of it. Thus a major part of the
petitioners' efforts at the U.N. must be expended in private
persuasions, and in these efforts Sherman, Emory, and I were
not much help.

The three Africans and Michael Scott worked for several
weeks without letup to round up support for a resolution that
would encourage or authorize resort to the World Court. They
received enormous assistance from a number of African delegations. Every day had its closed caucuses, its public affirma-
tions and private betrayals, its empty promises and unheralded
boosts. The jockeying about who would table what resolutions
and amendments, the maneuvering over words and phrases,
the threats and traps and bargains and soul searchings seemed
endless and are beyond summarizing. And of all this activity
not a line in more than a handful of American newspapers,
not a word in a magazine or a frame on TV. I wondered how
the American people could be expected to react to things they
could not, with the utmost diligence and determination, begin
to find out about. I wondered too at the infinity of activity
that must go on unnoticed beneath the surface flurries of press
releases and debates when issues considered major are dealt
with.

It seemed during those weeks that at any moment in any
corridor one might come upon Michael Scott buttonholing this
or that delegate or journalist, or engrossed in discussion with
two or three of the unsolicited helpers who seemed to appear
miraculously when needed. There was little money even for
clerical work, but willing hands always turned up to help with
mimeographing and other chores.

As the impression grew that Michael Scott had more or less adopted "the three Americans" for the duration of the session, we came to be sort of per stirpes beneficiaries of the loyalty and enthusiasm of his self-appointed aides, some of whom are extraordinary human beings. There were times when we would have been quite lost without the friendship and advice of these people and of representatives of groups like the American Committee on Africa and the International League for the Rights of Man. None of us will ever forget a remarkable woman, a member of a distinguished French family, named Anne-Marie Stokes, who has given up wealth and honors to work unpublicized, and often abused, for causes she holds dear. To us she seemed a sort of urban female Schweitzer whose buoyant common sense proved that the renunciation of worldly things need not include a renunciation of humor or of worldly wisdom.

At last even the time for lobbying had passed. On November 17, 1959, the General Assembly adopted the resolutions which had been recommended by the Fourth Committee. In doing so it took what was possibly its most significant step to date in the South West African controversy, for it approved, with only four dissenting votes (Australia, Portugal, South Africa, and Great Britain), a legalistic little paragraph freighted with anguished distant hopes. The operative paragraph of Resolution 1361 of the Fourteenth Session reads as follows:

"The General Assembly . . .

"Draws the attention of Member States to the conclusions of the special report of the Committee on South West Africa covering the legal action open to Member States to refer any dispute with the Union of South Africa concerning the interpretation or application of the Mandate for South West Africa to the International Court of Justice for adjudication in ac-

cordance with Article 7 of the Mandate read in conjunction with Article 37 of the Statute of the Court."

The overwhelming victory on the final roll call tends to obscure the fact that without the diligence, courage, and skill of a few devoted diplomats, most of them members of African delegations, such a resolution might never have been more than words in petitioners' speeches.

Above all, the passage of the resolution was due to the doughty efforts of Dr. Angie Brooks, then the Liberian Representative to the Fourth Committee and now its Chairman. Nothing could daunt this remarkable lady or turn her from battle till she had shepherded it through to final approval. When freedom comes to South West, it will owe much to the valor and diligence of many people, but Angie Brooks will be high on the list. Her contribution has gone largely unnoticed and unrewarded—she would not have it otherwise—but none of the petitioners who has tried to further the cause of South West Africa at the U.N. will soon forget his debt to her and to the government that made it possible for her to do so much invaluable work in the Fourth Committee.

In all, seven resolutions about South West Africa were adopted by the General Assembly. The ones concerning Hoachanas and Hans Beukes, each of which passed with only one negative vote and twelve abstentions, may be of particular interest. Resolutions 1357 and 1358 of the Fourteenth Session read in part:

"1357 (XIV). The Hoachanas Native Reserve
"The General Assembly . . .

"*Noting* that inhabitants of the Hoachanas Native Reserve . . . have an inherent right of ownership and possession of their ancestral land at Hoachanas, where they claim an area of

50,000 hectares as recognized by agreement with the German Government . . .

"Noting further that the Government of the Union of South Africa reported to the League of Nations in 1923 that it had confirmed the rights of 'Natives' on land occupied by them under treaties or agreements with the former German administration . . .

"Noting with concern that the Government of the Union of South Africa . . . caused the Reverend Markus Kooper and his family to be forcibly removed from Hoachanas on 29 January 1959 to a site approximately 150 miles away, thereby depriving his congregation of their minister, that several residents of the reserve were allegedly injured during the removal, and that the other inhabitants of the reserve were informed by Government officials of their impending removal by force,

"Considering with regret that it is the policy of the Mandatory Power to remove the 'Native' inhabitants from their lands which they have held as their own in order to make room for 'European' settlers, in violation of fundamental human rights and the sacred trust assumed by the Government of the Union of South Africa over the Mandated Territory . . .

"1. *Urges* the Government of the Union of South Africa to desist from carrying out the removal of other residents of the Hoachanas Native Reserve and to arrange for the return of the Reverend Markus Kooper and his family to that reserve;

"2. *Requests* the Government of the Union of South Africa to investigate the claims of the Rooinasie Namas to the original area of Hoachanas, of which only 14,254 hectares are now occupied by them . . ."

"1358 (XIV). Withdrawal of a Passport from Mr. Hans Johannes Beukes

"The General Assembly . . .

"Having received a report dealing with petitions from Mr. Hans Johannes Beukes, a South West African student, and from Mr. Neville Rubin, President of the National Union of South African Students,

"Noting that Mr. Beukes had been granted a scholarship by the Norwegian National Union of Students to study for three years at the University of Oslo . . .

"Considering that the Government of the Union of South Africa granted Mr. Beukes a passport on 15 June 1959 to enable him to proceed to Norway, and withdrew that passport on 24 June, when Mr. Beukes arrived at the port of embarkation, subjecting Mr. Beukes to a search of his person, luggage and personal correspondence . . .

"Taking into account that there are no facilities for university education in South West Africa and that non-European students from the Territory find it increasingly difficult to obtain adequate university education in the Union of South Africa,

"1. *Is of the opinion* that the withholding or withdrawal from a qualified South West African student of a passport for the purpose of studying abroad is not only a direct interference in the educational and general advancement of an individual but a hindrance to the educational development of the Territory of South West Africa . . .

"2. *Considers* the withdrawal by the Union of South Africa of the passport granted to Mr. Beukes to be an act of administration contrary to the Mandate for South West Africa;

"3. *Expresses the hope* that the Government of the Union of South Africa will reconsider its decision so that Mr. Beukes may take advantage of the scholarship offered him to study at the University of Oslo in circumstances permitting him to maintain normal relations with his family and his country."

The final paragraph of Resolution 1358 was added by a Guatemalan amendment whose wording was reminiscent of an intervention by the Norwegian delegate. Hans was particularly moved that envoys of nations should have remembered his personal situation in the midst of great international problems, and all the petitioners—especially those of us who had no previous experience in such situations—were constantly grateful for a flow of thoughtful gestures that minimized our awkwardness and helped modify our sense of presumptuousness. Nor shall we soon forget our gratitude for the patience and efficiency of the Secretariat, without which we would have spent half our time overwhelmed in procedural snafus and misunderstandings.

It was nice that the United States ultimately voted for the South West African resolutions in the Fourteenth Session; nice but not very significant, since the following year, despite the strong protests of Senator Morse and several other members of its delegation, it resumed abstaining on the most important of these resolutions. The American position was much improved in the Sixteenth Session, but there is still much to do to persuade suspicious Africans that amiable slogans no longer conceal an indifference to their problems, and that improvisation and perfunctory gestures no longer substitute for policy. The task will not be an easy one under the best of circumstances, for the speed of events in southern Africa does not leave much time to persuade anyone of anything.

Shortly after the adoption of the resolutions, I chanced upon Michael Scott in a corridor. He was surrounded by the customary fluctuating cluster of well-wishers, lost souls, volunteer aides, seekers of help for remote oppressed peoples, and stray characters curious to know what all the fuss was about. I overheard him say that he would be leaving the United States in a day or two, and managed to get his ear long enough to invite him to have a meal with the other petitioners away from the lobbies and coteries of the U.N.

And so there occurred one of those strange little farewells that punctuates the travels of diverse people gathered briefly in transit to the next cause. Michael Scott must hold the world record for such comings and goings, and as he begins another decade of dedicated wanderings they must blur in his recollection almost beyond the separating.

We gathered for supper on the eve of his departure to organize a protest against the French atomic tests in the Sahara. Everyone brought little going-away presents and tried to thank him for his kindness and guidance. Most of all we wanted to tell him how grateful we were to have been included in the kaleidoscope of transient souls whose lives are brighter and make more sense because of him. But attempts to say such things only embarrassed him into forgetting half his gifts, and soon we scattered to the next chapters in our separate lives: Michael Scott to the desert, Hans to his scholarship in Norway, Emory back to teaching at Milbrook, Sherman to Columbia Medical School, Kozo to scour first western Europe and then the communist world for help for his people, the Kerinas to take up the day-to-day struggle of conducting an international headquarters and a haven for escaped Africans in a tiny flat on a pittance of money.

A few weeks later Liberia and Ethiopia announced their intention of taking the case of South West Africa to the World

Court for a compulsory ruling, in compliance with Resolution 1361. The concept of world law would soon have its best opportunity to challenge injustice and lawlessness successfully.

But more than justice for South West Africa is in the scales. It is not likely that conditions in South West will remain as they are very much longer, whatever judges may or may not do; but neither is it likely that the creaking apparatus of international law will affect events anywhere if it cannot affect them in an international territory, or if it can be flouted even by the most isolated and friendless of governments.

IX There may be those who have become concerned about the situation in South and South West Africa and who wish to know what is being done to bring about a change—and what more could be done.

These questions are as complex as they are important, but it may be useful to glance at a few of the problems that beset groups seeking a change, and to discuss briefly in the last chapter some of the things that the outside world, and particularly the United States, could do to help South Africa toward a resolution of her problems.

Politics in South Africa is an intricate business, combining as it does the complicated trappings of a parliamentary system with the intrigues and perils of life in the Underground. Furthermore, activity on each level tends to proceed in ignorance of what is occurring on the other.

For the fifth of the population that is white the situation is rather as it might have been were they living in Germany during the rise of the Nazis. Various parties nominate candidates, denounce one another, and generally strive to carry on despite government-imposed liabilities that are explained as steps to suppress communism, and that coincidentally grow more formidable with the degree and vigor of opposition to government policies. Interruptions of personal freedom become more frequent and more ominous, sectional passions flare and subside, strident importunings to racial solidarity rend the air. Everyone sees one doom or another around the corner, and disagrees only on what to do about it.

Amidst all this, as one might expect, European interest in European politics runs high, for politics is Race, and Race is the national pastime as well as the national obsession. But it is an interest that borders increasingly on the irrelevant—blind men angrily choosing up sides to play earnest parliamentary games as doomsday closes in.

Meanwhile, the nonparliamentary four-fifths of the country seethes in back alleys and remote kraals, and gropes to determine leadership and direction much as such things had to be determined in Poland or Yugoslavia during the Nazi occupation. Racial, tribal, and language differences do not disappear overnight, especially with the government working hard to emphasize and exacerbate them.

Most nonparliamentary groups still talk about nonracial democracy as their goal, but there is increasing discord about what this means and how to achieve it. Disputes about whom to cooperate with, and for what immediate purposes, are in a flux as constant and ugly as the controversies about what techniques to employ. For the law in South Africa is so constructed as to thwart the orderly procedures by which men in a democracy can seek to change their government; and any who would seek such change here are obliged to search out and experiment with a twisted and conflicting range of other procedures.

Such a situation creates an infinite opportunity for disagreements and precludes the functioning of machinery to work them out. Frank discussion would be illegal and democratic decisions are impossible, so conflicts between contending views remain unresolved, or must be decided and redecided and decided yet again by stealth or violence. No one can know who "speaks" for whom. There can be no elections, no conventions, no reliable assessment of organizational strength. Even mem-

bership lists are precarious items: they must be kept somewhere, and by their very existence they invite betrayal by in-
formers and searches by the secret police.

Thus, the politics of the disenfranchised becomes a quag-
mire of frustration and division, further embittered by those
elections which are held. For these elections are conducted in
full view of those denied the right to participate in them, and
in fact usually revolve around the question of how to treat
those who have been excluded.

But even for white folk the voting is more a charade than
a process of choosing a government. The English press and
the parliamentary opposition condemn the elections as frauds
almost as vigorously as do the leaders of the disenfranchised,
for matters are so arranged that the Nationalists do not need a
majority of the popular vote to gain upward of two-thirds of
the seats in Parliament. The heart of the Nationalist program
for South Africa is of course apartheid, and whatever may be
said at the United Nations or in travel brochures for overseas
consumption, the purpose and meaning of apartheid is clear
enough to white and nonwhite alike at home. The Nationalist
Election Manifesto of 1958 put the matter simply: "The aims
of apartheid are: (a) the maintenance and protection of the
white people of South Africa as a purely white race and to safe-
guard its supremacy; . . ."

In practice the Nationalists obtain about half the vote cast,
virtually all from Afrikaners; and the government can thus be
said to represent at most one-half of the one-fifth of the population that is white. The M.P.'s elected by this fraction of the
country determine the fate of the whole, and such are the
rules of the Nationalist caucus that decisions can be made
by one-half plus one of the Nationalist M.P.'s voting by secret
ballot in closed meeting.

The official "Opposition" is provided by the United party, a disintegrating amalgam that long ago ran South Africa under Field Marshal Smuts. Its racial program, insofar as it has one, is *drift*. The devotion of its members to white supremacy is as ardent as that of the Nationalists, but being largely English-speaking their concern about world opinion is considerably greater. It seems senseless to the United party to antagonize much of the human race in order to satisfy charts and dogmas. Nonwhites could be kept in their place just as effectively, and probably for a much longer period of time, without codified superstructures that defy common sense and provoke outrage overseas.

There was a time when many non-Europeans hoped that the United party would return to power. A U.P. government, the argument ran, would produce at least a restoration of civil liberties and a shift of direction in racial affairs, in deference to world opinion if for no other reason. In such an atmosphere serious efforts to work out problems could be revived, and a hopeful interregnum might result. But most Africans have now concluded that the differences between the two major white parties are illusory, or at least balance out: the United party in office might be less vicious at home; it would surely be more convincing abroad.

And the recent behavior of the United party makes it difficult not to conclude that any shift it might undertake would be too slight and too late to avert disaster. Even the contention that a U.P. government would restore traditional personal freedoms has seemed dated since the days after Sharpeville, when the U.P. parliamentary delegation voted in the name of "national unity" for the Nationalists' sweeping repressive legislation. Thus the effecting of white solidarity has become more important to the "Opposition" than the defending of free speech or the developing of communication with nonwhites. And the price it must pay for such a priority is that it can no longer be said to offer a valid alternative to the present government.

For a time the lonely burden of parliamentary resistance fell to a small group of M.P.'s who bolted the U.P. and formed themselves into the Progressive party. The Progressives insist that South Africa must reverse course, and although they reject universal suffrage they would extend the franchise to "qualified" non-Europeans and govern in consultation with representatives of all races. Their fight against the "emergency" legislation after Sharpeville has brought them to the foggy jagged edge of what the government chooses to allow dissenting groups to do.

But the nonracial program of the Liberal party and the activities of militant non-European groups have helped to foster the impression that the Progressives are primarily oriented to the needs of the white community. They have therefore been able to develop a measure of grass-roots support among Europeans, and have obtained the financial backing of some of South Africa's most powerful commercial interests. On the other hand, many nonwhites who would never actively support the Progressives have been sufficiently impressed by the vigor of their opposition to Nationalist racial policies that a Progressive régime might still be able to negotiate a way out of the mess.

The Progressives today thus offer what may well be South Africa's last opportunity for a racial *détente*. Their candidates polled almost 70,000 votes in the European elections of October, 1961, although they contested only twenty-four constituencies. One Progressive, a lady of great energy and charm named Helen Suzman, won a seat in Parliament, and several others came close. But if this showing is not discouraging, neither should it obscure the fact that most South African

whites are still not prepared to consider any significant con-
cessions to the demands of nonwhites.

Nor will they be prepared to do this as long as it is possible to silence protests by repression and to ignore the ultimate
consequences of intransigence. And as discontent intensifies,
the continued intransigence of Europeans must find itself hand-
cuffed to a crescendo of oppression of non-Europeans. The
fiercer the oppression, the deeper the bitterness, and the deeper
the bitterness, the more desperate the efforts to bring change;
and so back to yet more oppression, and to the saddest fact of
all: unless the circle is somehow broken very soon the chance
for a Progressive accommodation will vanish even as have all
the others before it.

Across the chasm between white and nonwhite politics leap
or limp or sneak a handful of hardy idealists and intriguers,
themselves split half a dozen ways and doubtless bearing in
their midst the usual contingent of government agents.

The great majority of the European chasm-crossers who
are politically active are either members of the Liberal party
or communist sympathizers. The bitterness between these two
groups should be a familiar story to liberals and communists
everywhere, although the fact that in South Africa both are
predominantly white and are competing for nonwhite support
in the teeth of a hostile white government has produced a
grudging quasi-camaraderie. There are even spasmodic sus-
picion-laden truces.

Both liberals and fellow travelers proclaim nonracial democracy as their goal for South Africa. The Liberal party has
always solicited non-European members, at least until recently
without much success. The communists, however, since the
outlawing of the party itself, have operated largely through
uniracial "allied" organizations. The Liberal principle is doubt-

less the nobler, but in some ways the communist tactic has been better suited to conditions in South Africa. The structure of parallel organizations has allowed nonwhites to feel they are building and running their own groups, which then receive guidance and assistance from one another and from cooperative Europeans.

But the most envenoming of the differences between Liberals and communists in South Africa have derived from their orientations to affairs outside the Union; and about these affairs the non-European is understandably not very exercised. Yet the attitude of foreign powers *toward South Africa* is a matter of the greatest concern to non-Europeans, and in this connection the behavior of the Soviet Union has been an asset to its allies in South Africa.

The same cannot be said for the democracies, from which has come more financial assistance for the government than for its foes, and whose national policies more often than not have added to the burdens of pro-Western South Africans. For many years the American Embassy has excluded Africans from its social functions; the Soviet ignored the color bar, and gloated when its Consul General was expelled from the country. It is said that the United States has no choice if it wishes to remain on good terms with the South African Government; and perhaps this is true. But it does have *a* choice, indeed the same choice that the Soviet had, and surely it can be no wonder that the choices made have affected African thinking.

But the most useful ally the communists have had in their efforts to influence non-Europeans has been not the Russian Government but the South African, which persists in describing itself as the defender of Western civilization and Christianity against the Red menace. Not content to spawn conditions which invite communist success, the government has persuaded itself, as well as most Afrikaners and all too many non-Europeans, that any opposition to its racial policies must be communist or communist-inspired. Since the word "communist" means in the eyes of the law whatever the government wants it to mean, the atmosphere is as if McCarthy had had racial views more extreme than Eastland's and had controlled the Presidency, the Congress, and the jurisdiction of the courts to boot.

One of the government's signal contributions to the communist cause was the endless Treason Trial. The world is familiar with the outcome of this strange proceeding, which disrupted a thousand lives for several years before the special court selected personally by the Minister of Justice acquitted everyone whose indictments had not previously been quashed.

Less widely realized are some of the domestic consequences of this sad affair, which forced the ablest non-European leadership into a protracted intimate alliance with some of South Africa's shrewdest communists, gave the term "Red" wide currency as a synonym for treason against the apartheid government, and sustained a debilitating drain on the energies and funds of noncommunist opponents of the government. South African liberals could hardly abandon the defendants or their families. Neither could they maintain an adequate defense fund without abandoning important projects of their own.

And since the noncommunists were of course called communists for helping the defendants, their efforts to distinguish their motives and goals from those of some of the people they were helping had faint success among non-Europeans. With all the confusion that resulted from the government's profligate doling out of this sort of unearned credit to communists, non-Europeans can hardly be blamed if the sum of their impressions was that communists are the most dangerous foes of racial discrimination and that everyone concerned enough to help those arrested was likely to be a communist too.

In short, the meaning of "communist" has become over the years as blurred to the politically unsophisticated, African and Afrikaner alike, as it is in the "Suppression of Communism Act" itself. And communists benefit in yet another way from a situation grown so imprecise that anything or anyone opposed to apartheid (including the Roman Catholic and Anglican churches, the United Nations, and of course any nonracial opposition at home) is likely to be labeled Red at one time or another. For under these circumstances it becomes almost impossible to sort out the "statutory communists," who may be as far Left as the Archbishop of Canterbury or Herbert Hoover, from the Moscow-trained agents and the fellow travelers who have infiltrated and influenced many non-European political groups during the last decade.

For many years the communists were the only political party in South Africa that supported nonracialism. This, plus the bravado with which European communists have ignored or defied government threats, gave them a considerable start on less frenetic or less disciplined groups in the effort to influence nonwhite thinking.

The most extensive communist penetration has been in the organizations associated with the far-flung Congress Alliance, which consists of five separate units, four of them set up along racial lines. The affiliate for Europeans is a small front group called the Congress of Democrats whose impact on non-European politics has been significant, thanks to its close ties with the influential African National Congress (now banned) and the South African Indian Congress. Nor is communist penetration of the Congress Alliance limited to the influence of the COD, for some African Reds have achieved high positions in the ANC and some Indian Reds in the SAIC.

The ANC's most tangible link to communists derives from its use of a party-line tabloid as its unofficial mouthpiece. (This paper is suppressed periodically by the government, after which it reappears with a new name and greatly enhanced prestige among Africans.) Most ANC leaders are aware of the disadvantages of such an arrangement, but they see no alternative as long as lack of funds makes it impossible to have a publication of their own. Even the most liberal of the English press has viewed African political organizations with about as much enthusiasm and objectivity as a "moderate" paper in Jackson, Mississippi, would view the NAACP at the height of the sit-in season.

But when all is said and done, what is most remarkable about communist influence in the ANC is that despite everything it has never been dominant. Even the Treason Trial judges could find no evidence of communist control of the organization. The president-general of the ANC, Chief Albert Luthuli, was awarded the 1960 Nobel Peace Prize and is as devoted a Christian and democrat as any political leader in the world. His chief deputy, Mr. Oliver Tambo, is cut from the same cloth. Such men are dupes or pawns of no one. Indeed, it is hard to think of any political organization that has had two such high-minded and selfless individuals filling its top offices at the same time, and democracy, not communism, would be the winner were these men in power in South Africa.

There have always been strains between Europeans and non-Europeans within the communist hierarchy. These are not eased by the growing concern of astute African communists about conspicuous European participation in the resistance movement. The rising tide of black nationalism has a strong antiwhite backwash, and the notion is growing that continued rigid adherence to a nonracial line may cost the ANC its fifty-year primacy among Africans. For the first time in many years the ascendancy of the ANC faces a major challenge, and the key contention of the challenger (it too is now banned) is that no one but blacks can understand the suffering of blacks, so no one but blacks can be trusted to help end it.

The newer group calls itself the Pan African Congress to stress its kinship with all Africans and its claim of special ties with Dr. Nkrumah and other men prominent in the emergence of independent African states. The birth of the PAC was the outgrowth of a long series of ideological feuds and power struggles within the ANC, and was attended by a torrent of bitter charges and countercharges about who had frustrated democratic procedures where.

Most of the leaders of the initial breakoff were alumni of the ANC Youth Movement grown more impatient. In this sense there is some truth in the customary European description of the PAC as a "radical offshoot" of the ANC. If there was one theme common to the rebels, it was that the parent organization had grown too conservative, in techniques if not in goals. They blamed ANC's close relationship with Europeans for what seemed an increasing inadequacy of militancy, and since most of the ANC's European allies were communists or fellow travelers their opposition to working with whites often found expression as hostility to Reds.

It may confuse some Americans that many rabid anticommunists in South Africa are anticommunist because they are convinced that the international and interracial ties of communists prevent them from being militant *enough* soon enough. They are thus more antiwhite than anti-Red. But it is also true that unhappy experiences with European communists have helped turn them against cooperating with any whites.

The eastward drift of Guinea, Ghana, and other centers of Pan-Africanism has further complicated the PAC's anticommunist posture. Indeed, Dr. Nkrumah, among other PAC heroes, is widely believed to be urging forcefully a reuniting of the ANC and PAC. Events after Sharpeville did produce a wobbly "United Front" among nonwhite exiles, but it is hard to see how even a theoretical and surface unity can sur-

vive in London or Accra while the infighting at home grows
more savage.

PAC politicians, confronted with the difficulties of competing for a rank-and-file against an organization with prestige
accumulated over half a century, have adopted as a campaign
slogan what was in any case an organizational tactic: only
blacks are welcome in the liberatory struggle. But this, it is
explained, is a tactical decision and does not mean that the
PAC is antiwhite. They talk of all white men as members of
the "ruling class" and refuse to admit them to membership,
or even to work officially with any non-African group. On the
other hand they insist that whites will be welcome in the new
South Africa if they care to stay on as equals.

It is not easy to estimate the strength, let alone the relative
strengths, of the ANC and PAC, especially now that both
have been outlawed. Most urban Africans do not feel involved
in the intramural squabblings and at heart are ANC or PAC
as the occasion merits: whoever is currently striking the most
effective blow at white domination will get their support.

There is little organized political activity among rural Africans, whose procedure for expressing their feelings about the
present order of things is to burst more and more frequently
into riots. The fact of the matter is that while theoreticians
and tacticians haggle over the merits of passive resistance in
the urban areas, the countryside has long since fallen into
other ways. The ferocity of repression keeps pace with the
frequency of the disturbances, and although it is easier to conceal events in remote Reserves than in more accessible places,
what evidence is available suggests that the government's
brutality in some of these areas dwarfs Sharpeville.

The most vivid eyewitness account of what transpires in a
Reserve during a police occupation has been provided by the
Reverend Charles Hooper in a book called *Brief Authority*.

His experience was in the Bafurutse Reserve near the town of Zeerust; the more recent occupations of Sekhukuneland and Pondoland appear to have been even nastier. At any event there is already a monotonous familiarity to the order of events: passes are decreed for women or tribal chiefs are deposed for rejecting the Bantu Authorities Act, disorders greet the pass issuers or the government-appointed chiefs, mobile columns are dispatched and borders sealed. Then all is silence till refugees begin to appear in Bechuanaland or in neighboring Locations or at the outposts of harried missionaries.

To the average urban African talk of cooperating with whites seems mostly a trap: the benign white man lives as richly as the malevolent one. How many men relegated to the nether regions for no reason but their color could accept as sincere the fraternal protestations of those who return from every interracial tea to the heaven always visible and always just out of reach? And even if such protestations are accepted as sincere, how many could accept them as adequate?

So the black man wonders: How can you trust the honeyed words of those who denounce apartheid and enjoy its fruits? Is this white man a spy? Is that another group of Europeans eager to control Africans for their own purposes? Even the least objectionable kind of white helpers, the victims of troubled consciences, are more trouble than they're worth: the sense of guilt may be genuine, but it will never be strong enough to overcome racial ties in the omnipresent vagary of a "showdown." And who is to know what enthusiasm such people may dampen or what plans they may betray at such a time?

Nor has it eased suspicion that noncommunist Europeans have rarely seemed content to cooperate on an organization-to-organization basis. Often they have appeared to regard their admission to a particular African group as a test of its nonracialism. That granting such membership might weaken the group seemed impossible to most Europeans, or at least irrelevant. And that their own willingness to forego such membership could be to Africans a test of their commitment to the common cause was inconceivable.

Yet overt cooperation with Europeans can pose serious tactical as well as philosophical problems for African politicians. I shall not soon forget a discussion that erupted at a meeting of African leaders to whom I had suggested a project that might greatly increase overseas support, but whose success would depend on African unity and might require the use of occasional Europeans in high positions. Everyone agreed that the project could have great value, but the idea of using Europeans provoked an impassioned debate which coursed this way and that as if I were not present.

There was the same turbulent urgency to the arguments, the same scrambled conflicting and blending principles and pragmatisms that so torment European liberals. Emotional and practical considerations lapped up against one another and lured and countered each other in confused rhetoric:

—No white man suffers the adversity, so why should any white man be given a place of importance? Let him work in the ranks if he wishes to work with us at all.

—Let him work in his own ranks. I do not trust him in ours.

—It is not that the white man would ask to be important but that we may need one or two to be important at this time, for *our* purposes. And if there are any we can trust it would have to be one of the outstanding ones, and such a man would be wasted in the ranks.

—But suppose all else fails and we must go on to other tactics—where would such a man stand at such a time?

—But it is not that time, it is this time, and if we work wisely now we may never come to that time. It is senseless to weaken ourselves now by fears of theoretical defections at some future point that may never come.

—The man in the street would never accept such a thing. He would feel betrayed, most of all if we did it.

—Surely that is nonsense if it hastens the liberation by increasing heavily the overseas assistance; and anyway if all African organizations were in this together there could be no charge of betrayal.

—Ach, man, we have been hearing of this overseas assistance for years, and the most that ever comes are a few words at U.N.O. We can rely on no one but ourselves; we weaken ourselves to take in others.

—But now there are new states in Africa, independent states, and every day there are more, and they have votes at the United Nations and soon they will have armies just as the European powers have. And this man says America is waking to us, too, and if America wakes these things can be changed overnight; overnight, man. . . .

—Ach, America is a big country, very rich, and very far away. She will not concern herself with our affairs here and we will have nothing to show but confusion and bitterness for thinking such thoughts.

—But this project might help to concern her. Are we to give up without so much as a try at it? What could be more help to the government than such thinking?

—How long truly will it be before we get help from America? If we support such an effort and work in it with Europeans?

And so they were back to me, but still I said nothing further lest I affect the decision here more than I could affect the follow-through later. At last the chairman called for a show of hands, and all but two voted that they would approve the project even if it meant agreeing to European participation.

Then one of the dissenters turned on me and said, "You

have won your vote on the theory of it—now find such a European who can thus be trusted with the lives of all my people!"

Against the background of African attitudes and political complexities, it is not difficult to understand the dilemma in which European liberals have long floundered. Denied access to Africans in Reserves without unobtainable permits, suspicious of the ANC's ties to fellow travelers and resentful of the PAC's attitude toward non-Africans, many whites eager to make common cause with Africans found themselves able to do so only with whatever Africans joined the Liberal party. This, relatively few Africans have been willing to do, partly because of the urgent needs of their own organizations, but in large measure because of the Himalayan variance in viewpoint and status that inhibits and complicates relationships between even the most sympathetic European and virtually every African.

In recent years only the Liberals of all South Africa's political groups have tried to compete on both sides of the parliamentary abyss. The contesting of an election here and there has seemed sensible to most European Liberals, even though there is no prospect that the party will ever carry a white constituency. The presence of a Liberal candidate on the ballot affords ordinary voters a chance to be counted anonymously, and the campaign itself offers relatively sheltered opportunities for propagandizing: it is awkward to arrest candidates in the midst of an effort to prove that elections are free. Most Africans, on the other hand, regard any participation in white elections as an acceptance of the validity of these elections and an indication of ultimate loyalty to the white man's institutions. A European who votes while non-Europeans are unable to do so invites the resentment that comes when a man seems to enjoy special privileges even as he denounces them.

Thus even procedural questions can cloud trust across racial lines; and every major philosophical and tactical issue is faced on both sides in a great bog of tension and misunderstanding.

The liberal European is obliged to live and hopes to be effective in a white racist constituency. His goals are the goals of men of good will everywhere. With minor quibbles they are the stated goals of non-Europeans in his own country. He would attain these goals by the law-abiding methods of reasonable men who are so devoted to the ways of a free society that they find it almost impossible to act on the implications of their own pronouncements that South Africa has become a police state.

His hope has been that non-Europeans would identify with his goals, appreciate his sincerity, and trust patiently to his techniques, while Europeans would come to accept the inevitability of a new social order and value him more and more as the most gentle of its midwives. Thus even in a franchise limited to whites the liberal vote totals would gradually climb, while the outcasts cheered.

His problem has been that things tended to work out backward. Those excluded from Parliament grew cynical about those pledged to pursue noble goals by "parliamentary means"; while intransigent whites, unenthusiastic about black domination however achieved, have increasingly regarded any white who took such a line as a potential Trojan horse. Caught building a bridge both shores would prefer to see blown up, liberals have been so pressed defending the bridge itself that incursions onto solid land have been muddled and ephemeral.

This is a quandary far more complex than the customary pull between principle and expediency that besets humanitarians facing the realities of politics. It is principle versus principle, and expediency versus expediency, and round and round again, with no end in sight. What, for example, should the liberal position be on universal adult suffrage?

This may seem at first a rather distant issue. It is nothing of the sort to most Africans, or, for that matter, to most Europeans. Is the applicable principle that all men are created equal and shall be so acknowledged in the voting booth? Or is it that democracy cannot survive without an informed electorate, and that the franchise shall accordingly be limited, not by race but by educational and other standards of achievement? And what is the higher expediency: to sacrifice all hope of winning European converts by supporting "one man, one vote," or to destroy any incipient rapport with blacks by rejecting this slogan that is anathema to whites?

Surely reasonable men will note that this is not an immediate problem, and some compromise can be worked out which would satisfy both principles and both expediencies. For instance, how about the *ultimate* adoption of a universal adult franchise?

There may be some confusion at this point about where principle ends and expediency begins, but assume for the moment (as many would deny) that the addition of the word "ultimate" does no violence to liberal conviction. How would such a solution fare pragmatically?

Perhaps rival white politicians should be asked not to declaim henceforth that "universal" still means "universal," that betrayal and doom still thunder through the phrase, that soft soap does not cleanse a Trojan horse. They may not be so obliging; but surely on the opposite shore, among the non-whites, such a solution will fare better. And it might have, fifteen years ago. But today there are twenty-eight independent African states, and successful mass illiterate voting in India, and fifteen years more of proof that the very literate white man cannot govern democratically right here at home.

And there is more. There are the white men of the Congress of Democrats preaching "one man, one vote" without equivo-

cating evasions; and there are articulate, irate black nationalists
inviting the white man to leave if he cannot live as an equal on
the black man's continent.

How do you compete with Reds if you first hand them a
loaded revolver and then place your brains neatly at its muzzle?
How do you check the growth of African alienation and its
tempting doctrine that no white man can understand black
aspirations, if you first qualify your support of the most basic
of these aspirations? And how do you preach democracy if you
limit its applicability when it might result in a nonwhite majority electing a nonwhite majority to Parliament?

But if so rational a solution loses support among both black
and white, clearly one must choose sides. And how do you do
that without abandoning the highest principle of all—the
principle of nonracial cooperation fording all the gulfs of skin
and language to keep open at least some channels of communication?

The Liberal party has long since endorsed universal adult
suffrage in principle, but to many individuals the conundrum
seems ever deeper, the maze twists unendingly, and wise men
go on discussing philosophy even as they see the absurdity of
discussing philosophy while angry lava singes their feet.

The dilemma of the white liberal is even more excruciating
at the countless junctures where words become either action or
hypocrisy. At such junctures the white man is suddenly confronted by a forgotten corollary of the disparity between white
and black living standards: the disparity of sacrifice entailed
in making the commitment to seek the overthrow of the established order.

For the black man who has little or nothing, little or nothing
may be lost by carrying on opposition activities in a way not
sanctioned by law. To the comfortable white man, the risk of
going beyond words seems disproportionate to any possible

contribution. After all, the fight can be waged better by men at large and with access to their considerable properties than by a few more political prisoners rotting unnoticed in a Johannesburg cell.

How many mortals finding themselves in a paradise of material comfort would choose to trade it all for a term in prison to prove the depth of their devotion to racial justice? A courageous few may criticize so unfair a system of deciding who gets to Paradise and who watches in misery; the penalty for such outspokenness is likely to seem sacrifice enough: political oblivion, social ostracism, officially sanctioned slander, periodic raids on home or office, and loss of passport.

To go further—to leave the relative sanctuary of verbal protest for the tangled no man's land of extralegal activity—is to invite personal ruin; and to what end? It takes a great courage and a conscience outraged beyond endurance to overcome the temptations to compromise that come with a luxury as beguiling as the South African white man's.

Even to remain active in the Liberal party has required such a courage and such a conscience since the arrest of nine party officials after Sharpeville. For if these arrests had any meaning at all (no charges were ever made against those arrested), it had to be that the mildest sort of dissident activity is no longer safe in South Africa.

And so for the liberal European these are the hardest times. Plagued by his conscience and jailed by the police, pilloried by most whites and rejected by most nonwhites, sniped at by fellow travelers and deserted by the Western democracies, he retreats into silence or flees into exile or advances out to more exposed positions as circumstances and character dictate. Perhaps the most remarkable fact about South African liberals today is that there are any; and perhaps the saddest portent for South Africa's future is that there are not a great many more.

A footnote should be added about Coloureds and Jews, two groups that exist in an insecurity so pervasive that it has intimidated vast sections of the Coloured and Jewish communities into inertia. The analogy between Coloureds and Jews is of limited value, for Jews are white and Coloureds are not; and this of course is the controlling fact of life in South Africa. Furthermore, the status of Coloureds is fixed by law and is generally enforceable by visible criteria; and these things are not true of the situation of Jews in South Africa.

Nonetheless there are some interesting parallels. Both Coloureds and Jews are comparatively well off on their own side of the color bar, a fact that gives rise to considerable jealousy among stronger groups in less privileged situations. Neither feels certain how long its relative good fortune will be tolerated, and neither is sure whether its greater danger is from white or black nationalism. Both have been seared enough by discrimination to abhor it, and to dread arousing more of it against themselves.

The inference that people who have endured racism are unlikely to relish it has reinforced Afrikaner prejudices with the suspicion that few Jews or Coloureds can be counted on to stand by the government. Indeed, both groups produce a lively pepper of militant and often radical crusaders against the established order.

Such troubadours of discontent may tap the vein of idealism in their neighbors; they also undermine whatever fragile sense of security has been fashioned out of the largely unreciprocated efforts to identify with more powerful elements. Thus, each outspoken opponent of the government seems a threat to his embarrassed and frightened peers, whose profoundest hope is to be left alone and who rush to dissociate themselves from him as best they can.

It is, of course, not unnatural for Jews to feel insecure in a country whose Minister of Justice was the leader of a pro-Nazi underground during World War II, and whose Prime Minister sympathized publicly with the Nazi cause. The government insists that it is not anti-Semitic, and Jews have recently been allowed to apply for membership in the Nationalist party; but it may not be unfair to infer something about Dr. Verwoerd's attitude from a celebrated letter he wrote recently to a Jewish lawyer in Cape Town. The Prime Minister made sour comments on a vote cast by Israel against apartheid at the U.N., a vote for which he apparently holds South African Jews at least partially accountable; and followed these comments with this rather odd remark: "The fact that during the last election so many Jews have favored the Progressive party . . . did not pass unnoticed."

The Prime Minister denies that this letter should be considered a threat against the Jewish community. "If I want to threaten the Jews of South Africa I will not do it privately. I will threaten the whole lot of them," he announced at a Nationalist party conference.

A noted South African rabbi recently deplored the behavior of Jews in South Africa as "the abdication of a community," but if it is true that the bulk of the Jewish community nurtures its whiteness with hothouse care, it is also true that man for man the record of South African Jews is far better than that of other white religious groups. Disproportionately large numbers of Jews have chosen to support movements opposed to apartheid, and have continued this support despite all the inducements and the great pressures to conform; and much of the outstanding European leadership against white supremacy has been Jewish. No general roster of such leadership could omit Helen Suzman, the only Progressive now in Parliament, and one of South Africa's most effective woman politicians; or Sam Kahn, the last communist M.P., and Leo Lovell, one

of the last Labour M.P.'s; or Solly Sachs, her most notable
trade unionist; or Ronald Segal, the brilliant editor of a now
defunct magazine called *Africa South;* or Ellen Hellman, the
tireless dynamo of the South African Institute of Race Relations; or Leslie and Neville Rubin, who vexed the government
almost in tandem while Neville was president of NUSAS and
his father one of the four Europeans representing Africans in
the South African Senate; or any of innumerable others.

The educational and social standards of Coloureds, especially in Cape Province where the vast majority live, are closer
to those of Negroes in the United States than those of Africans
in the Union. So, for that matter, is their pigmentation. They
are spared much of the unofficial hell of the Africans by a
curious quasi-respectability which discourages police wanton-
ness and wards off a good deal of the arrogance of individual
Europeans.

But all in all the position of the Coloured population is a
pathetic one. For these are a people who have always prided
themselves on being "brown Afrikaners," who share the Afrikaner's language and religion as well as his blood lines. For
centuries they were accepted as an appendage—proud, poor,
trusted, unchanging—of the Europeans; the magic blood of
European ancestors swims in their veins, and this was cause
enough for a shared franchise, an exemption from the perils of
the pass system, and even for the privilege of talking back on
occasion.

Then came the Nationalist government of 1948, apartheid,
and the removal of the Cape Coloured voters from the common
roll. Professor Gwendolen Carter, perhaps the outstanding authority on South African elections, has concluded it is doubtful
that Coloured votes changed the result in any parliamentary
constituency; in other words, the emotional impact of the removal was far greater than its political. For the first time a

South African Government—and an *Afrikaner* Government at that—had told the Coloured community what it had long managed to avoid facing: black blood is not neutralized by white blood.

This message has since been reemphasized by successive legislative enactments: Coloureds are as excluded from European universities as Africans, and are as fenced around by the Job Reservations Act, which limits and stratifies employment opportunities by race. The Group Areas Act, which immunizes cities against contamination by non-Europeans, is to be applied to Coloureds no less than to Africans.

Nor should the effect of the Population Registry Act be forgotten: every South African must now carry an identity card obtained after his racial category has been determined by investigation. The workings of such a law are harshest on persons in the insecure middle, whose lifetime identification with one group is subject to sudden undoing at the whim of some minor bureaucrat. Alfred Hutchinson expressed a general reaction to the classification procedures in his book *Road to Ghana:* "I wouldn't submit to the classification tests if they tried. I would never, I told myself, never. They wouldn't stick pencils in my hair and ask me to bend my head to see if the pencils would stick or drop off. I wouldn't allow them to comb my skin for tribal marks. I wouldn't allow them to punch or knead my nose to test whether it was Coloured or African. I wouldn't allow them to pinch my ears nor would I answer questions. I would have nothing to do with the body of 'pass office anthropological tests' that had grown up. I had told them my ancestry and that was enough."

The government's attacks on Coloured status produced a peculiarly bitter irresolution in the community. Some Coloureds made full cause with other opponents of white supremacy, but a sullen rationalized neutralism became the prevalent mood. An undercurrent of almost lugubrious self-pity developed: to the whites we're black, to the blacks we're white; we're doomed if we do and doomed if we don't, so do nothing, swallow your pride, make no enemies, and maybe we can hang on to what we've got for a while longer. Resentment against Europeans ran high, but the hangover of snobbery toward Africans is strong; as is the dread of losing the economic and social appurtenances of being a rung or two higher on the racial ladder.

But slowly the notion is taking hold that rejected appendages are not very popular with anyone, and that if Coloureds can never be whites, perhaps they had best try to be blacks; or at least try to be accepted by blacks. Coloured leaders have taken to warning that rudderless acquiescence invites further repressions by Europeans, while indifference to the plight of other non-Europeans multiplies African and Indian resentment. There has been a spurt of political activity, and the extent of Coloured participation in the stay-at-home of May, 1961, may indicate that timid despair will soon have run its course as a group posture.

If such reactions can be sustained, and if they can be channeled into alliance with other non-Europeans, the effect on South African politics could be far-reaching, for the active cooperation of the bulk of the Coloured community would add great resources of funds and leadership to the extraparliamentary opposition.

That any effective cooperation has survived the differences and difficulties that beset nonracial South Africans is due to the overriding hatred of the government, and to the efforts of a few remarkable men.

Some of these men have attained national preeminence despite personal preoccupations with the affairs of a particular organization. If the energies of Chief Luthuli have been expended primarily through the ANC, his influence in keeping the ANC to nonviolence and nonracialism has in turn had repercussions through all of South African life. Similarly, Robert Mangaliso Sobukwe, the head of the PAC, is a man of the profoundest integrity and intelligence who has striven to prevent tactical disagreements from driving his organization into perpetual sullen hostilities with other opponents of the government. And it is hard to believe that the Liberal party, with its great value as a bridge and as the vanguard that helped prepare the way for the appearance of the Progressives, could long exist were it not for the efforts of Alan Paton, who has been its national president and indomitable rallying point.

But there have also been a few extraordinary men who have stood apart from the factionalism of opposition groups, who have managed to be of it all and yet somehow to stay above it all. Perhaps the most valuable of these men for over a decade was Dr. Ambrose Reeves, the Anglican Bishop of Johannesburg and the pivot who pulled things together, insofar as they could be pulled together. His fate tells the story of the course of events since Sharpeville, and provides as good a clue as any to the shape of things to come.

No good cause, no suffering individual, no frightened victim of some government policy hesitated to seek help from this man whose great energy and wisdom sparked and guided and challenged wherever he went. Were there mass arrests in Sekhukuneland? The bishop would find money to defend the accused. Were students protesting the closing of their universities to nonwhites? The bishop would be there to inspire, and to forfend by his presence any further abominations. Was there a famine in the Transkei, or a dispute among rival groups about a boycott in the Transvaal, or a threat of mass evictions of 60,000 Indians in Durban? See the bishop—the bishop would know what to do—the bishop would get money, or speak out, or soothe clashing points of view.

Like everyone else in need, we had made our way to the bishop's house. We arrived there on a mild afternoon of the Johannesburg winter expecting to find an imposing ascetic, harassed and sad-eyed under the weight of events. The bishop's children were playing tennis with an assortment of people of various ages and races, and we were taken in hand by Mrs. Reeves, a lady of such kindness and insight that no visitor could long feel unwelcome or uneasy. Soon the bishop himself appeared, a warm, chipper, sparrowlike man bearing a tray with tea things. It could have been a carefree Sunday in any pleasant suburb in England or America, if one could forget the secret police posted at the entrance to the estate.

What made the bishop peculiarly dangerous to the government was that his effectiveness was not limited by racial or political lines. But what most outraged the government was this ordinary, daily aspect of his activities. As long as he was around, there was an eminently respectable place in Johannesburg where men of all races could meet and play tennis while young people laughed and human intercourse proceeded with a naturalness that is taken for granted in more civilized places.

The bishop's doings placed the government in one of its most awkward dilemmas. Could it jail a high official of a major Christian church and still represent itself as a bastion of Christian civilization? On the other hand, how long could it leave at large a man who had become virtually irreplaceable as the funnel, mediator, spokesman, and inspiration of an opposition in chronic chaos and in desperate need of precisely such a funnel, mediator, spokesman and inspiration?

Furthermore, the way in which this dilemma was handled would have implications far beyond the fate of an obstreperous bishop. For Ambrose Reeves had come to symbolize, and to galvanize, European resistance *within the law* to the government's racial policies. In the rush of events, such resistance, or even all resistance by Europeans, might prove ineffective or inadequate; but was it to be made illegal?

For some years the government growled, muttered, tapped wires, and opened mail, but Bishop Reeves continued to function. Then after the shootings at Sharpeville the bishop and two young attorneys, Ernest Wentzel and John Lang, collected and released to the overseas press a number of depositions from survivors. These depositions provided the outside world with eyewitness accounts of what had happened; they also appear to have pushed the government too far. Or perhaps the bishop and his attorneys were simply caught up in the sweep of precipitate government actions induced by the general post-Sharpeville panic.

Be that as it may, Wentzel and Lang, both of whom were leaders of the Liberal party, were jailed without bail or charges. They spent four months in prison, presumably for the crime of attending to the legal business of clients. The bishop, on the other hand, was ultimately deported, a procedure the government must have thought very clever at first blush, for it removed him from the scene without incurring the stigma of having jailed an eminent churchman.

The loss of Bishop Reeves was of course a grievous blow to opponents of the established order, but its long-run consequences can hardly strengthen the position of the government. The world cannot help noticing that in South Africa today it is unsafe for a Christian bishop to practice his religion; and it cannot help wondering who may practice such a religion when bishops may not.

To deport Ambrose Reeves is to announce that it is not violent change the government fears, but any change, and that it is just as illegal and intolerable to seek the downfall of

apartheid by speech and example as it is to seek the same ends
by revolution. Such an announcement can only hasten the replacing of nonviolent, nonracial leadership with more desperate
men. It must widen the chasm between races and viewpoints
and assure the evolving of other means of bringing about
change—means that may prove even less attractive to the
Afrikaner minority than interracial tennis parties and outspoken pronouncements by bishops on the meaning of Christian love in a troubled society.

Of all the things the government has done to hasten the dis-
integration of South Africa, perhaps the least rational has been
this persecution of the few men whose presence could remind
the victims of apartheid that injustice is not a matter of race,
and whose influence among such victims was exerted on behalf
of nonviolence. Such men do not grow on trees, and when one
such is silenced it may be a decade before another appears
whose eminence is sufficient to affect the thinking of despairing
people.

But now there are no decades left. There are only frustrated
masses cheated of their last avenues of peaceful protest, and
fanatical defenders of a dying order poised Samsonlike by
the pillars of their own temple. And one day soon it may be
clear that the irreplaceability of the Ambrose Reeveses and the
Albert Luthulis and the Oliver Tambos has become an even
greater problem for the supporters of the government than for
its opponents.

X   It is the thesis of this book that the present state of affairs in southern Africa is as immoral as any in the world today; that the internal opposition to this state of affairs has been stalemated, and will turn in desperation to a long-range campaign of violence unless massive outside assistance is forthcoming soon; that the situation is deteriorating, not improving, and that a change of direction must be achieved quickly if there is to be any hope of avoiding the frightful consequences of a denouement by blood; that in view of these facts the situation constitutes a grave threat to the peace of the world; that united action by the international community is the last chance to bring about a peaceful and humane resolution of this situation; that such external intervention is justified morally and legally, and could in practice be successful without the use of force; that the United States must take the lead in applying outside pressures, both for the sake of their effectiveness in South Africa and for our own sake as leader of the free world; and, finally, that the problem of southern Africa is building rapidly into one of the most dangerous of the crises demanding the attention of the American people.

One of the questions I was asked while we were testifying before the Fourth Committee concerned the possibility of outbreaks of general violence in South West Africa. The Summary Record reports my reply as follows:

"Mr. Lowenstein said that the situation in South West Africa was more explosive than was thought. That did not mean that the indigenous inhabitants were ready to revolt, or that any responsible African leaders believed in violence as their means of seeking a change in government. On the contrary, the last words of Chief Hosea Kutako to the United States petitioners before [Mr. Lowenstein's] departure had been an eloquent plea for love and peace. But the indigenous inhabitants seemed as determined to oppose the plans for removing them from Hoachanas and from the Windhoek Location as the Union Government seemed bent on carrying them out. . . . It would be wrong, therefore, to dismiss the possibility of violent outbreaks for which the international community would bear the responsibility owing to its failure to bring sufficient pressure on the Union Government to live up to its sacred trust."

Two months later word came that there had occurred in the Windhoek Location one of those periodic massacres that the South African Government contorts into evidence of native contentment and proof of South Africa's reliability as a bastion against communist penetration.

The story was a familiar one: impending mass evictions of Africans are announced, the objections of those to be evicted are ignored, a crowd gathers to protest, nervous policemen fire into the crowd. But this time I knew the people involved. How often, and how recently, I had met with their leaders to try to figure out how, and to whom, voteless people without legal protection could appeal against being moved about like chattels.

Mr. Eric Louw subsequently informed his Parliament that there would have been no disturbances had it not been for our visit. The Administrator of South West Africa agreed that "outside agitators" were "one hundred per cent" to blame. Such is the habitual announcement of South African officials when

confronted with African unrest; they do not agree with what
Bishop Reeves has called the "elementary fact" that agitators
find it extremely difficult to stir up a contented people. But on
this occasion, since we have been identified as the "agitators"
in question, it may be worth recording a few other facts about
our meetings with the leaders of the Windhoek "disturbances."

What difficult, almost pathetic, meetings they were for all of
us: grown men hiding and whispering to avoid being overheard
in discussions about how to protect their homes! Always the
central concern of the discussions was how to avoid violence.
The Africans were certain that any protest they might undertake, however peaceful, would be turned by the police into a
pretext for bloodshed. I had doubted that anything more
damaging than tear gas would be fired into an unarmed crowd;
it had seemed far more likely to me that if blood were shed it
would be because repeated frustrations had temporarily deranged crowds of Africans. Accordingly, it was the problem
of restraining black tempers, not white trigger fingers, that had
engaged our greatest attention. But black tempers had been
restrained, and now eleven people from the Windhoek Location were dead and at least fifty wounded.

I wondered what this had done to black tempers. And I wondered further what there was left to say for peaceful protests.
For it is of course the fact that although it takes both parties to
a dispute to avoid violence, it takes only one party to import
it. The testimony of Lieutenant Colonel Pienaar before the
commission that investigated the shootings at Sharpeville helps
to explain why the police so frequently import it. Lieutenant
Colonel Pienaar is a veteran of thirty years' service in the force
and was in charge of the units at Sharpeville. "The native
mentality," he said, "does not allow them to gather for a peaceful demonstration. For them to gather means violence."

Photographs taken at Sharpeville recorded the amiable, almost lethargic, mood of the crowd, and the presence of great numbers of women and children. The medical evidence established that of 253 dead and wounded Africans, more than 70 per cent had been shot from behind. Lieutenant Colonel Pienaar was asked if he had learned any "useful lesson" from the events at Sharpeville. He replied, "Well, we may get better equipment."

In point of fact, the most practical lesson the police seem to have learned was that shootings cause an international revulsion disproportionate to their value in South Africa. Thus, when Africans called a stay-at-home in Cape Town a few days after Sharpeville long leather horsewhips had replaced guns, and policemen patrolled the streets of the city and invaded neighboring Locations *whipping* whatever Africans they happened upon en route. They happened upon thousands. Before the whipping was over, Cape Town was out of bandages and Africans were filled with as much terror and hatred as if another massacre had taken place. But horsewhips exacted nothing like the same price in shocked headlines overseas.

Sharpeville and its aftermath reflected and hastened the collapse of order in South Africa. In fact, men may soon be saying that Afrikaner nationalism attained its apex and began its final plunge on the same day, May 31, 1961, the day on which the Republic of South Africa was born. A glorious birthday it seemed at the time to Afrikaner Nationalists: not only was the foreign queen dethroned, but a political strike designed to dramatize nonwhite discontent was crushed as well.

The organizers of the strike had called on non-Europeans to stay home for three days. Their most specific demand was for a multiracial convention to discuss possible new approaches to South Africa's problems. The government reacted by mobilizing its military forces, arming white civilians, jailing ten thousand Africans, banning public meetings, raiding the places of its opponents, and patrolling urban areas with fleets of armored cars—in short, by placing the country in a state of siege. Simultaneously the ties to the Commonwealth were formally dissolved.

This was a combination of events almost unique in the experience of modern nations, for it is not often that the birth of a new state coincides so perfectly with the estrangement of its last friends abroad and with the deploying of an army of occupation to hold down most of its own people.

Despite the elaborate precautions of the government, and the poverty and eternal feuding which hobble all non-European efforts to organize, a considerable number of people did in fact stay home at first, including many Coloureds and Indians. Not enough stayed home, however, to shield those who did from reprisal, and by May 31st almost everyone had returned to work. Thus, the Republic could announce at its birth that everything was "normal," an announcement which told a good deal more about normalcy in the Republic than was intended.

African leaders came to the conclusion that the mass jailings and the collective memory of Sharpeville were the factors most responsible for the splotchy response to the strike. The splotchy response thus assumed a Pyrrhic significance for the future of the Republic, for it drove many nonwhites to the unwelcome conviction that traditional forms of nonviolent protest cannot be effective as long as the government not only can arrest anyone it wishes to arrest but is prepared as well to shoot down large numbers of peaceful Africans. Under such circumstances non-Europeans have only two choices: to acquiesce indefinitely in the present situation, or to seek new methods of effecting a change. Anyone who chose acquiescence would not last long as a leader.

Furthermore, the patience of victims of tyranny has a habit

of running out without regard for the strategies of their leaders or the cluckings of sympathizers in distant places. It is running out in South Africa, where misery will soon explode. And so a macabre timetable now hovers over discussions of South Africa's future, for almost everyone accepts, in theory if not in implication, the inevitability of an "explosion" of some sort.

If the explosion is violent it will be because the world outside, and especially the United States, permitted nonviolence to fail. If it is anti-West it will be because the present government has sustained itself by courtesy of the West. If it is anti-white it will be because white men failed for so many long years to oppose convincingly that which is antiblack. As things are going now it is likely to be all three. And we shall have only ourselves to thank if we have done nothing until it is too late to do anything but count corpses and court hostile fanatics.

Americans turned to violence to gain independence after other means of redress had failed. It should come as no surprise if South Africans are beginning to plan for revolution against a far more opprobrious government. Nelson Mandela, the chief organizer of the May 31st protest, told the South African press early in June: "If peaceful protests like these are to be put down by mobilization of the army and the police, then the people might be forced to use other methods of struggle."

The behavior of the outside world seems designed to encourage recourse to other methods, for apparently only the shedding of blood stirs much interest, whether in Angola, the Congo, Cuba, Vietnam, or South Africa. And the central fact about South Africa has become that every day finds non-Europeans more determined to begin fundamental changes right away, and more convinced that the old methods will not bring such changes.

Although everyone speculates about how soon violence will come to South Africa, what is really meant is how extensive unplanned African violence will become and how soon planned African violence will begin. For it is plain that violence itself came years ago, when outbursting non-European throngs and nervous European policemen began their fateful interplay. Blood has been shed, and more blood will be shed, at protest meetings and in spontaneous rioting. Protest meetings are no longer to be permitted, but spontaneous riots do not depend on permits and may in fact be said to flourish when the permits required for other forms of expression are denied.

What blood has been shed so far in South Africa has resulted more from circumstance than from design; and very little of it has been the blood of Europeans. This situation too is due to change. No non-European politician, however militant, welcomes the prospect of an extended campaign of violence; the contending forces are too unequal, the inevitable damage too great. But now hope for freedom is focused on the outside world, and indifference there to nonviolence at home has become a powerful incentive to violence: surely *someone* will have to step in if civil war starts. And if no one should do so, such a war revives at least a distant hope, for in the long run— much longer than Kenya, or even than Algeria—there simply are not enough white men to prevail over black men at the foot of the black man's continent.

Thus is coming now to the most peaceful of Africans the turmoil of reexamining old commitments and of acquiring new and distasteful skills. The soul-searching will take time, longer for some men than for others. So will the new kinds of training, and the formulation of new plans. But these things are now in progress, and the dwindling interval of this transition is the last chance to avoid a blood bath that could become one of history's most dangerous and least necessary catastrophes.

Planned violence will start with modest projects involving industrial sabotage. Soon terrorists will strike at isolated white farmers reputed to have mistreated African labor. Once such things are underway in earnest, they can hardly fail to multiply themselves in succeeding horrors. The reaction of Afrikaner Nationalists leaves little to the imagination, and to meet this reaction each of several embittered groups would set out to prove itself the toughest and most ruthless opponent of white supremacy. Most liberal Europeans will long since have fled (the exodus has already begun); and among non-Europeans "moderation" will soon seem disloyalty: the more bloodthirsty the leader, the more trustworthy his leadership. Communists, black racists, religious fanatics and political opportunists, gangsters, and countless individuals angling for power or glory will vie for control of an increasingly ugly and chaotic situation. These are not circumstances in which the voice of reason or the scruples of the democratic conscience are likely to prevail.

Nor is it whistling up fantasies to anticipate such a sequence of events, for even now South Africa is leapfrogging into mayhem. At least two secret organizations committed to the violent overthrow of the government have been put into operation, as has the government's program to tighten its noose around its opponents' necks. Soon the total authority over black men possessed by the President of the Republic as "Supreme Chief" of all Africans is likely to encompass all non-Africans as well, and anyone who has gained the disfavor of the Minister of Justice will need a permit if he wishes to *sleep* at a house not his own. What retaliation will such regulations evoke from men already turned to violence? And how long can so unequal a struggle go on before outside help is solicited?

Independent African states might be the first to send help, but inevitably one group or another will seek assistance from

Russia and China. It would be foolish to suppose that "volunteers" as well as equipment will not be made available at propitious moments; just as it would be foolish to suppose that the spirit of Mau Mau and of Lidice could be prevented from engulfing South Africa in twin floods of atrocities such as distinguish wars of revenge.

There are many in the West who would insist in such a situation that the way to head off communism in southern Africa (and to save the white race) is to intervene on the side of whatever coalition the white rulers are able to put together. Considerations of morality quite apart, it must be clear that the choosing of sides along such lines could hardly hurt the world communist movement, even if fighting were to be localized; if it were not localized, the survival of the planet itself could be imperiled. It should be noted in this connection that the South African Government has announced that it is now able to develop its own nuclear weapons.

The prospect of rival outside interventions fanning a race war in Africa is a dismal one, but it is hard to conceive of any united procedure the international community could agree to follow once matters have been allowed to degenerate to this point. It may be a mystery why the Western democracies have done so little to avoid such a situation; there can be no mystery why some other powers which denounce "racism" and "imperialism" do not seem very disturbed at the prospect of international inaction continued for several years more.

Thus more than moral indignation impels the urgent pleas for immediate steps by the United Nations to bring the present régime to its knees. For what happens now in South Africa is up to the outside world. There are risks to doing anything; there is a greater risk to doing nothing.

More accurately, in this situation to do nothing is tantamount to doing a great deal. Not to boycott is to trade;

not to withhold recognition of all-white groups is to buoy such groups with the international status that means so much to people fearing isolation. (Is there any excuse in this day and age for allowing teams based on racial exclusions to compete in the Olympics?) Every new investment of outside capital, every renewed failure to help those who would change South Africa's direction, is *ipso facto* an intervention against change.

In short, the issue is not whether to intervene, but how forcefully and to what end. Alan Paton has written:

"There is one hope, and one hope only, for the future of the white people of South Africa, and especially for the Afrikaner, and that is to come to some kind of terms with the other thirteen million; to negotiate, to discuss; to increase, not to decrease, representation; to open the door, to unload the guns; to stop these stupidities like not shaking hands; to renounce the evil laws that result in violence and death, to foreswear apartheid.

"Can the Nationalist do it? Can he give up being boss? Is there some terrible and irrational compulsion in him that is leading him to death? We are all asking these questions. . . . One thing is certain: he won't change just by persuasion, or out of the goodness of his heart. He will change only when the pressure inside and outside the country becomes unendurable. . . . It is the United Nations that may need to come to our aid, and to give support to those who are concerned with building a nation and not with racial revenge.

"I am not convinced that the Afrikaner Nationalist, like Samson, will consent to his own death. Yet he is as blind as Samson was. . . .

"What he needs to bring him out of the pipe-dream is a decisive order from the outside world. It must be an order to bring to an end the second greatest Christian apostasy of the twentieth century, or to take the consequences.

"Many of us pray that such an order will soon be heard."

To hesitate further to issue such an order is no favor to the South African white man. In Peter Ritner's words: "When all is said and done we are trying to save the lives of the white settlers, not hurt them."

Since a major purpose of planned African violence will be to arouse outside assistance, such assistance made available immediately and in adequate measure might avert such tactics. But there is much to do and very little time in which to do it.

The democratic opposition must be supplied with financial and moral support commensurate with the scope of its task, and organizations abroad which support this opposition—the Africa Bureau and Christian Action in England, the American Committee on Africa and Episcopal Churchmen for South Africa in the United States, for example—should be given greatly increased support. A counterpart of Radio Free Europe should be beamed at southern Africa. A nonracial university should be established, preferably in one of the Protectorates, where facilities would be available to train substantial numbers of non-Europeans in the professions and for public service.

Most important, the international community must exert the kinds of pressures, including sanctions and boycotts, that would quarantine South Africa; for the value of outside assistance will be minimal unless it induces the sort of fundamental reassessment by Europeans without which there can be no voluntary change in South Africa's course. Even the Progressives, who decry "meddling" for the benefit of the white electorate, know that without the prospect of increasing meddling their support would shrivel overnight.

If such a reassessment can be brought about without civil war, a nonracial democracy might yet emerge in which the fundamental liberties and legitimate interests of all men could be protected. Many men in many places would be eager to underwrite such protection. On the other hand an interregnum of civil war would have to end, when finally it did end, with the victorious race too bloody, and too inured to bloodshed, to worry very much about the abstract rights of its own people, much less those of a hated, dying foe.

The Afrikaner Nationalist has grown used to justifying his conduct as essential to self-preservation. It may not be too late to transform his great drive to preserve himself into an ally of the effort to arouse his conscience to the rights of other groups with drives and needs not so different from his own.

There are those who deny in the name of realism that non-violent pressures, whether internal or external (or both), could produce such an about-face, let alone bring down so well armed and ruthless a government. Nor is it certain that they could. It is, however, certain that they have yet to be tried, and that nonviolence in South Africa is foredoomed without massive support from abroad.

In any case, to refuse to support nonviolence on the theory that it cannot succeed is simply to guarantee its failure. To refuse such support and offer no other is to suggest to the dominant group that the *status quo* can go on forever, if only it will hold to defiant postures; and is, at any rate, to invite those who are kept down to turn to other weapons. How long can the outside world insist that South Africans must be nonviolent at the same time that it excuses itself from supporting nonviolence on the grounds that it is futile against the South African government?

If peaceful measures fail it will be time enough to consider more drastic steps. But is it not in the best interests of the United States and of the U.N., as well as of South Africa, to do everything possible to try first to resolve the mess in southern Africa with a minimum of violence?

Those who oppose sanctions as ineffective like to cite declarations by various white South Africans to the effect that external hostility further entrenches internal intransigence: as if the Turks at Gallipoli had announced that if the British attacked once more they would have to surrender. Men threatened with a siege rarely announce in advance their inability to withstand one. Their best (or only) defense may well be to dissuade the enemy somehow from mounting one.

As long as most Europeans believe they can hold onto everything they now have, they can see no reason to look for ways to hold onto less than everything. And nothing that has happened within South Africa has revised this belief.

The record suggests, however, that South Africa is particularly vulnerable to siege. For one thing, the national income depends heavily on foreign trade; but which countries would stand up for South Africa against sanctions invoked by the United Nations and backed by the United States? And how long could the South African Government stand alone once the world united against it on behalf of three-quarters of its own people?

Whatever Dr. Verwoerd's inner circle may think about the matter, and however often defiance is declaimed from on high, each new sign of isolation brings new wobbles in the constituency. Pressures from outside have so far been halting and disorganized; but paltry though they have been, Afrikaner intellectuals already have begun to reexamine their approval of apartheid, Afrikaner businessmen have begun to talk out loud about conferring with non-Europeans, and more than 70,000 whites have voted for candidates pledged to an early end of white supremacy. Moreover, no less a personage than the Minister of Transport has acknowledged that South Africa is faced with its most difficult economic situation in fifty years, and that the country would be in a bad way if foreign boycotts were to gain momentum.

But much more must be done at once if there is to be any chance of South Africa shifting directions peacefully. And the shift would have to be very different in tempo and emphasis today than would have been necessary ten, or even five, years ago, or even until May 31, 1961; for there is now a long way to go just to get things back where they were a few years ago, and the impatience and bitterness of the nonwhite population have multiplied in the meantime. Thus the longer South Africa continues on her present course, the more difficult a transition becomes. Changes have to be increasingly drastic to meet the mood and needs of her Africans; and to Europeans these changes seem even more drastic than they are, for demands are replacing requests even as thoughts of revenge are replacing thoughts of cooperation.

So a spirit of last-ditch resistance mounts among the ruling Europeans, and with it the brutality of nonwhite repression. And then some cite this as reason to delay rather than to hurry the start of the transition, as if the inflicting of more outrages by whites while in power somehow justifies slowing their downfall, because these outrages are likely to weaken the spirit of moderation among their victims.

If the representative assembly that opponents of white supremacy have been demanding were to be held soon, it should still be able to hammer out a program that all but the diehard *colons* could live with; but the task becomes more formidable with the gathering of more and more strength at both extremes. If such a program were to be agreed upon by any sizable spectrum of South African opinion, the international community would have to be prepared to underwrite it, to guarantee the rights of minorities, and to assist with the relocation of any who might wish to leave.

The new group of displaced persons—displaced in this instance by their own choice—would, after all, be a relatively small one as such things go. Afrikaners like to assert that they alone have no home but South Africa; but their insistence that persons of Indian descent are "unassimilable," and therefore remain Indians no matter how many generations removed they may be from any connection with India, sets a standard for determining who is to be considered a South African that is not without pertinence for the future. There are, of course, other bases than race for establishing who is and who is not assimilable.

To gain a consensus of support among South Africans of all races, a program would have to include at least the repeal of legislation enforcing racial separation where individuals or groups do not wish to be segregated; the repeal of the pass laws, and the opening of government bureaus to help find employment for men needing work; the adoption of an escalated floor under wages that would raise African income above the breadline immediately, and to a decent minimum as swiftly as possible; the turning over of responsibility for South West Africa to the Trusteeship Council of the U.N.; and new parliamentary elections based on a nonracial franchise which might retain for the time being some educational qualifications.

Steps such as these taken in conjunction with the adoption of a Bill of Rights and the resettlement of those unable to accept racial equality could make for a relatively painless transition to democracy in South Africa. Which is like saying it is relatively painless to lose a cancerous lung—relative to dying, or even to losing a leg, but still requiring surgery and still unpleasant, and by no means guaranteed to end the peril of further cancers or the need for further surgery. But people who have breathed hatred for many years, to tax the metaphor, should not be surprised if there is malignancy in their breathing apparatus.

There are people who cannot bring themselves to support

measures against racial injustice elsewhere as long as all is not as it should be at home. Opposition to injustice elsewhere is no excuse for ignoring or excusing it at home; but neither do domestic shortcomings provide an excuse for doing nothing about racism running rampant abroad: as if Americans had had no right to boycott Hitler because mobs have lynched Negroes in the South and Sigma Chi had a restrictive clause.

Surely the individual conscience is not supposed to be restrained by national boundaries, and is free to balk at injustice wherever it may be found. And surely individuals may seek to make their indignation felt even when governments do not. But in any case there is no comparison between the racial oppression in South Africa and that in other parts of the world.

To say this is not to minimize the import of conditions in America, but rather to note that here the law and the power of the nation are firmly on the side of equality; and that in any event the United States is not in the process of imposing white supremacy on unhappy nonwhites outside her borders.

One can grow just as weary in Johannesburg hearing about the sister who must be saved from marrying the irresistible black man as one can in Birmingham. But beyond a few such slogans and the white attitudes that underlie them there is little similarity between the situation in southern Africa and that in the southern United States. The fact that each new racial atrocity in the United States encourages South Africa's misbehavior should provide added incentive—as if any should be needed—to speed progress at home. But to insist on perfection here before doing anything about South Africa is to make of our imperfections a handy rationalization for acquiescing in far greater injustices elsewhere.

There is also opposition to sanctions based on the theory that sanctions would in practice increase the suffering of those whom they are supposed to assist. And so they might, at first.

The point is that an oil-less South Africa bereft of her overseas markets would not long be able to avoid economic ruin. Non-Europeans would often be the first to lose their jobs, but the damage to the high standard of living of Europeans would not be far behind, for the plushness of the white man's South Africa depends on the exporting of gold, diamonds, uranium, and other commodities. Only a threat to this plushness seems to the non-Europeans to offer any hope for a change in the white man's attitude, and under these circumstances most non-Europeans regard the likelihood of temporary further declines in their situation as a minor consideration. Virtually without audible dissent they have pleaded for the strongest possible economic and social quarantines, and have even mounted sporadic boycotts within South Africa itself at considerable inconvenience to themselves.

The United States usually replies to these pleas with expressions of sympathy and assurances that we are in a better position than people in South Africa to decide what strategy is best designed to bring them relief. Then we applaud another resolution deploring racial oppression and discover various reasons for being nice to the oppressors, one of the chief of these being that in some mysterious way such behavior is for the good of those who are oppressed.

Patrick Duncan, the son of a former Governor General of South Africa and the editor of a liberal journal called *Contact*, warned recently against this kind of response. "Since under an increasingly Nazi-like government," he said, "normal methods of open political opposition will become decreasingly possible, the West must either play a part in supporting unconventional opposition or leave the field to the communists."

The story of Jariretundu Kozonguizi is a case in point. This dedicated and high-minded person was sent by Chief Kutako to seek help for the people of South West. He came first to the United States, where he found that many of those to whom he had turned for assistance considered themselves the allies of those who oppressed his people. He then joined the parade of frustration to Moscow and Peiping, the first South West African to do so. He will not be the last.

In China he spoke angry words about the "Free World," and when he came back to the United States it was said that this proved he is a communist and that his cause is therefore inimical to the interests of the Free World. Jariretundu Kozonguizi insists that he is neutral about the cold war and that his only concern is about the plight of his people. He cannot see what place the struggle between East and West has in Africa, but he will take help where he can get it to bring freedom to his homeland.

And that is the only way that communism could come to southern Africa: not with Marxist slogans nor by subversion, but as the champion of democracy, as the source of help for beleaguered people seeking something better than what has been.

Michael Scott talked to the Fourth Committee last year about the changing mood of some of the non-Europeans of South West: "Can it be wondered at if they begin to look after fourteen years of debate and procrastination—however misguided we may believe some of them to be—toward those who have always been held up to ridicule and hatred by their oppressors?"

If suffering people ask us to help and we refuse, are the suffering people then to blame if they seek help elsewhere?

Recent developments in South West Africa suggest that matters there may be closer to disaster than in South Africa itself. Many Africans have made their way out of South West since our visit, and their evidence, as well as reports sent from the scene, indicate that conditions are now worse than ever and are deteriorating rapidly. Fighting may spread south from Angola, where the border splits the Ovambo people, or may erupt independently in South West at any moment. Could the civilized world stand by if armed white men began slaughtering the people they are supposed to be "protecting" in an international territory?

Mr. Nathaniel Mbaeya left South West on May 2, 1961. His report is typical of those of many other recent refugees. "The people of South West Africa," he said, "are prepared to be killed for their country. If they were armed, the explosion could have occurred two years ago. The situation is so bad, however, that they might revolt at any moment even though they have no arms. The situation is very tense. Africans are threatened not only by soldiers. Every European represents a threat. When a white man puts his hands in his pockets, an African might fear being shot and assault the white man. The Europeans themselves expect an explosion; that is why they are armed."

The 1961 report of the Committee on South West Africa reflects alarm at the decay in the situation and calls for "intervention" by the United Nations, including the application of "compulsory measures within the purview of the Charter": "The Committee . . . has been able to gather invaluable information which once again confirms the unbearable conditions under which the Territory is being administered by the South African Government. . . .

"The Committee concludes that the South African Government, through its application of the apartheid policy and of related . . . measures which establish the rights and duties of various sections of the population on the basis of their colour, race and tribal origin, its failure to promote and protect the rights and interests of the indigenous population and of the Territory as a whole, its denial to the Native population of all basic human rights and fundamental freedoms . . . and generally by its exercise of powers of administration and legislation in a manner inconsistent with the international status of the Territory, has violated its obligations under the Mandate and the Charter in relation to South West Africa. Indeed, all of this is conclusive proof of the unfitness of the South African Government to continue further with the Mandate. . . .

"The Committee is convinced . . . that the continuing application of the apartheid policy in South West Africa and the continued defiance by the South African Government of the authority of the United Nations over the Mandated Territory have created such a deep-seated resentment among all Africans and such a tense situation that *only intervention by the United Nations can prevent armed racial conflict.* . . .

"The Committee draws attention to the fact that the Mandatory Power has encouraged the arming of the European population of the Territory and has established military fortifications and large defence forces within the Mandated Territory, and has at the same time revised the integrated military programme of the Territory and South Africa to provide, among other things, for a Citizen Force of wartime strength and a speed-up in the production of arms and munitions.

"The Committee, after a careful appraisal of the extremely delicate and explosive situation in the Territory of South West Africa, came to the conclusion that, in view of the unfitness of the South African Government further to administer the Territory, the best interest of all concerned and of international peace and security demand *as a matter of great urgency* that the General Assembly should undertake a study of the ways and means by which to terminate South African administration over the Mandated Territory of South West Africa and to have that administration assumed directly or indirectly by the United Nations. . . .

"The Committee is convinced that, short of *compulsive measures* within the purview of the Charter, the problem of South West Africa cannot be solved in present circumstances in a manner that will protect the lives of the indigenous inhabitants of the Territory and ensure the maintenance of international peace and security in Africa. . . .

"The Committee, in accordance with its findings and conclusions, makes the following recommendations: . . .

"(*a*) [to create] the conditions for restoring a climate of peace and security:

"(1) Urgent consideration by the Security Council and all other organs, sub-organs or Member States of the United Nations of all such measures or courses of action as may be required to ensure the effective implementation of the recommendations made in this report. . . .

"(2) *The immediate institution of a United Nations presence in South West Africa;* . . .

"(5) Training and organization of an indigenous police force by the United Nations, withdrawal of firearms from all Europeans and prohibition of the possession of arms by all civilians, withdrawal of South African military forces, abolition of all discriminatory laws and regulations, and cessation of all organized immigration of Europeans, especially South Africans, to the Mandated Territory.

"(6) Attainment of independence by South West Africa through a Constitutional Convention, a popular referendum on the constitution adopted by the Convention, the election of representatives of the people on the basis of universal adult suffrage, the establishment of an independent Government— all with the assistance of the Committee on South West Africa or the suggested United Nations Special Committee of Assistance to South West Africa.

"(*b*) [to take] steps which would enable the indigenous in-

habitants of South West Africa to achieve a wide measure of
internal self-government designed to lead them to complete
independence as soon as possible:

"(1) Immediate organization of a special, intensive type of
fellowship programme to train the largest possible number of
indigenous inhabitants of South West Africa in the functions
and techniques of administration, economics, law, hygiene
(sanitation), etc., increasing thereby the available number of
trained personnel of indigenous background;

"(2) The planning . . . of preliminary drafts, *inter alia,* for
the following:

(*a*) A Constitutional Convention;

(*b*) A popular referendum . . . ;

(*c*) Educational system;

(*d*) Economic organization;

(*e*) Agrarian organization and reform, particularly on
the question of land ownership by the indigenous
population;

(*f*) Technical and economic assistance by the United
Nations and its specialized agencies"

[Author's italics.]

United Nations committees do not speak lightly of employ-
ing "compulsive measures." Nor do they lightly recommend
"the institution of a United Nations presence" in remote places
under unreceptive rulers. When the United Nations Committee
on South West Africa, whose staff includes some of the world's
foremost authorities on South West and whose members have
just concluded an intensive study of developments there, urges
such steps it would seem unwise to proceed as if nothing very
pressing were amiss.

The South African Government has made it perfectly clear
how it will react to any effort to station a U.N. presence in

South West; it will not even permit a handful of U.N. delegates
to pay a brief visit to the Territory in the course of writing
a report. If South Africa can defy the world community in so
urgent a situation involving an international responsibility and
get off with resolutions expressing displeasure, is there any hope
of ever building an international organization capable of establishing the rule of law enforceable against great and small
powers alike? One need not condone the impotence of the U.N.
in other situations to fear the consequences to it of a continuing
abdication in the face of an urgent report of its own committee.
Surely if the U.N. can send armed forces against Katanga it can
use economic pressures against South Africa!

The problem of South Africa's behavior in South West
should be of special interest to people who are convinced there
is ample moral and political justification for moving against
the South African Government but who nevertheless have
strong misgivings about predicating international action on the
"internal affairs" of a country. To many of these people, even
the threat to the peace that inheres in whites exploiting blacks
in Africa is an inadequate legal basis for intervention.

In view of the situation in South West, there is no need to
debate the validity of such misgivings, for surely there is no
legal impediment to moving against the Union for its *external*
transgressions. And he who knowing about the situation in
South West still finds procedural reasons to stay neutral invites
the suspicion that his circumspect legalisms merely cloak approval of or indifference to brutality and international lawlessness.

Thus the tragic rush of events in South West can be turned
to some good, if we will it so. It can help to minimize the far
greater tragedy now threatening all southern Africa and preparing to spill out beyond. And in any event it is coming to be
the litmus test that will confirm the credentials or expose the

pretensions of those who protest their devotion to justice and human freedom.

Just as some object to the use of sanctions against South Africa on the grounds that they would not be effective, others object on the grounds that they would be. And these objections should be faced squarely, for they raise fundamental questions about the purposes and strategy of American foreign policy.

Many people find it incomprehensible that the United States does not do everything possible to buttress the present South African government. A few, like the Legislature of the State of Mississippi, which voted to congratulate the Union Government on its handling of the Sharpeville affair, specifically approve of South Africa's racial policies. More often the argument is that these policies are not our business—we have our own race problems in any case—and that South Africa is the only reliable anticommunist bulwark in Africa.

Mr. Anthony Harrigan, Associate Editor of the *Charleston News and Courier,* put this point of view forcefully in a series of articles which appeared in a number of American newspapers. Mr. Harrigan's first article was a report on an extensive interview with Mr. J. J. Fouche, the South African Minister of Defense:

" 'South Africa offers strategic advantages as a springboard' for freeing the African continent of communism. . . . Defense Minister J. J. Fouche thus characterized the military significance of the nation that controls the southern tip of Africa. . . . He added that his government does not foresee Lumumba-type regimes taking over Portuguese territories in East and West Africa while Portugal is a member of NATO.

"Mr. Fouche also stressed that any Fidel Castro type of communist invasion of South West Africa, a territory administered

by his government, 'certainly would be detected and re-
pelled.' . . .

"Mr. Fouche cited close cooperation between South African
and other free world naval forces. In naval exercise CAPEX
last year, he said, a sea training operation was carried out by
units of the United States, British, French, Portuguese, and
South African navies. . . .

"In considering the military resources of the free world in
its resistance to communist expansionism on this huge continent, South Africa is a strong and vigilant sentinel of the
West."

The last article in the series began with another interview,
this one with Mr. H. J. Klopper, Speaker of the South African
House of Assembly:

"The speaker came from behind his desk and, stabbing a
finger at my chest, said: 'I want you to tell your Americans that
we shall fight communism here in Africa. We shall fight it no
matter what you in the United States do, whether you are with
us or against us.'

"Nowhere else on the African continent could one find a
political leader who would make such a statement. Not one
of the so-called 'emerging nations' will make a flat declaration
to resist communism. And yet South Africa, which will fight
to keep the Reds out of the strategic southern tip of Africa, is
reviled in the American press and voted against by the U.S.
delegation in the United Nations.

"Here is a country that gives a safe harbor to U.S. ships; that
permits the U.S. to base planes on its territory to track missiles
from Cape Canaveral; that allows the U.S. to construct a space
probe telescope; that buys American automobiles and other
goods; that trusts in American integrity and fair-dealing, and
that sends planes to fight with the U.S. against the Chinese

communists in Korea. And yet South Africa receives nothing
but abuse in return.

"If South Africa, like Ghana, Egypt, Sudan and other African states, were to declare itself neutral in the cold war, if it
were to begin flirting with the Russians, immediately the United
States would be forced to attempt to buy its friendship as it is
seeking to purchase the loyalty of lands to the north.

"But South Africa isn't seeking a dollar from the United
States and never has done so. . . . It is openly and totally
committed to the cause of Western civilization.

"Americans who realize that South Africa is the United
States' best and only true friend on the African continent can
only wonder at what forces shape the State Department's policies. . . .

"When the United States votes with the communist bloc and
neutralist nations against the interests of South Africa, the
United States votes against its own security.

"Nothing in Africa is more important in the cold war than
keeping sea communication around the Cape of Good Hope in
Western hands. Of equal importance is keeping South Africa's
tremendous industrial machine on the free world side. If
revolution should take place in South Africa, or if that country
should be plunged into racial chaos, the only industrial power
in Africa might fall into communist hands.

"Stirring enmity against South Africa is the No. 1 African
objective of the communists. They know that so long as South
Africa is free and in the hands of Western people, it will be
a threat to their new colonialism in Africa. . . .

"South Africa is the key to the future of Africa and the one
absolutely essential ally for the United States on that continent. In all likelihood, it is the only nation in Africa that has
a destiny as a major power. The reasons are clear: a European population with high standards of education, tremendous

investment in science, mineral riches, abundant lands for growing food, a free press, established parliamentary government,
and a vigorous national way of life steeped in the values of the
Christian religion. . . ."

The amount of support for this attitude toward South Africa
is greatly increased by people who do not share Mr. Harrigan's
reasoning but who agree nevertheless with his conclusions.
Such people do not like the present government very much but
hesitate to oppose it for fear of what might take its place. Some
of these say that the present government, whatever else it may
be, is stable, and its downfall will bring disorder; others feel
that in the context of the world crisis, it is unwise to weaken
any government whose opposition to Soviet expansionism is as
emphatic as South Africa's.

These arguments, though beguiling, seem at best short-
sighted in the extreme. For disorder is already on the way,
under the worst possible circumstances for everyone except
communists; and experience should have taught us by now
that to abet an unpopular pro-West dictatorship is the best
possible way to increase the probability that its successor in
office will be anti-West. Nobody knows what will take the
place of the present government, but it is clear that someday
soon *something* will; and what that something is will be determined largely by how it comes to power—with whose help, by
what techniques, and after how much more suffering.

No one would dream of suggesting to the people of eastern
Europe that they should be quiescent, or even grateful to their
oppressors, in the name of helping along the cause of freedom.
But this is precisely what it sounds like we are saying when we
tell people suffering under oppression outside the iron curtain
to be patient because, after all, things under the Russians are
really worse.

Reports of murders in Hungary can seem rather irrelevant

to nonwhites in southern Africa: how would Hungarians respond if told they should support the Soviet Union because it is vigorously opposed to a tyrannical government in South Africa? Moreover, such reports often are simply not believed —are regarded, in fact, as the propaganda of racists eager to discredit those opposed to racism.

Statements like some which have been attributed to the head of the U.S. Information Agency in South Africa do not help the cause of freedom in South Africa, or for that matter anywhere else. As recently as May 2, 1961, in the midst of the various preparations for the birthday celebrations of the Republic, this official of the American Government saw fit to hail the South African Government "for the steadfast manner in which it opposes communism. . . . America and South Africa," he said, "must stand closely together against the communist danger."

This sort of remark has its counterpart in many parts of the world. It is usually amplified by a bow to the democratic conscience in the form of assurances to the victims of the local tyranny that while the local tyrant may be bad, the new imperialism of Khrushchev is infinitely worse; as of course it is, in a global context and in many specific areas. But Khrushchev replacing Nagy in Hungary is a far cry from Khrushchev replacing Verwoerd in South Africa. And it is dangerous self-delusion, as well as inaccurate sentimentality, to go on believing that the black majority in South Africa is better off under Verwoerd than it would be under the "new imperialism." At any rate, no African is going to believe it.

It is time we tried to understand the bitterness of people held in bondage on our side of the iron curtain in deference to the "practical considerations" of the cold war. It is small consolation to those people to hear that because of the urgent communist threat the miseries of South Africans or Angolans are of secondary importance, for we need the help of their oppressors in a greater struggle. South Africa is not of secondary importance to the South Africans; nor is it to a vast community of non-Americans around the world who measure the sincerity of our preachments by our performance at home and in other places where support of liberty may not always seem to coincide with our own immediate convenience. Conceivably the demands of defending America's freedom require that some others live in servitude; but if this be the case we should at least have the grace not to lecture such victims of our needs about their indebtedness to the "Free World."

Democracy's strength is that to her, decency is universal. Her concern must be about the rights of *all* people. But even if we ignore ethics and discount public opinion as a force in world affairs, we had better weigh carefully the military and sociological fact that to support any tyrant is to court the hatred of the people whom he is oppressing. If the right to use certain facilities as military bases is important to the security of the United States, it seems foolish to bank on keeping these rights by supporting governments whose days are numbered, when the price of so doing is to alienate the people who will be making the decisions about such matters in the long run.

Nor does it follow that people whom we have helped to freedom would be likely to return the favor by refusing to cooperate against newly-recognized threats to their freedom. But when we support noncommunist tyrannies in the name of defending the "Free World," we define the issue in a way that must encourage the oppressed to throw in their lot with the most powerful visible alternative to this kind of "Free World." How many times must we spawn Batistas before we realize that Batistas inevitably spawn Castros?

The danger of this approach to the world situation has been spotlighted in Angola, where the American people are constantly told that they are faced with a terrible dilemma.

But what exactly is the terrible dilemma? Is it a moral dilemma? Can it be that we don't know if it is right for a small European dictatorship to keep distant colonies under its rule when the people who live in the colonies revolt? Or don't we know if we believe that brute force, including the use of American weapons, is an appropriate method to suppress such a revolt? Or is the dilemma that we don't know whom to believe when 150,000 refugees and a wide range of journalists and fleeing missionaries charge that a system of slavery is being maintained by a country which professes outrage at the charge but erects an iron curtain to prevent inspection of conditions under its control?

Or is it a dilemma of practicalities: perhaps we can't decide whether the Portuguese Army or the Angolans will ultimately win out; or perhaps we don't know if it is more important to keep a base in the Azores or to strive for the goodwill of the nonwhite peoples of the world.

What sort of equations are these? If such things really drive us into terrible dilemmas—even if we end up casting occasional votes at the U.N. against the Azores—can we really expect that such an attitude will not be reciprocated whenever the nonwhite world decides how it feels about our positions on other matters, from Berlin to nuclear testing?

Our natural proclivity for hailing as our allies in the "Free World" anyone who favors us in our contest with the Russians should provide a clue to the test that others use in determining who their allies are to be in their own contests. Is our perspective so warped that we can't understand how others are going to view our struggles if we are indifferent, or neutral and calculating—and not even calculating intelligently—when it comes to theirs? And if we support the Portuguese dictator in the name of the Free World against the rebellion of his slaves, where do we expect the slaves to try to get help against the so-called Free World? Can't we support our fundamental principles even when moral and practical considerations join to make urgent demand that we do so?

There is another aspect to the fear about what might replace the present régime in South Africa. This aspect is not directly political, for it grows out of the racial nature of oppression in South Africa; but it has melancholy political implications for the United States. Its roots are in the lingering double standard that has given America a shoddy record in race relations at home and has encouraged the suspicion that we are less concerned about the sufferings of nonwhite people than we are about the sufferings of people who are white.

This double standard is so subtly a part of many of our attitudes that often it is as unnoticed as it is ingrained. It insinuates itself into discussions about South Africa when one white man asks another if he doesn't understand "as a white man" how terrible it would be to be ruled by blacks; and into discussions about Africa when someone asks if Africans are "ready" to govern themselves—as if you or I, or in any case someone *not an African,* has somehow acquired the right to make such decisions for Africans.

It is present when we decide that our slogans about "majority rule" do not really apply where a presumptuous nonwhite majority is not content with whatever beneficences a generous white minority may decide to extend. Actually, the silent thought goes, white civilization *is* superior, and is it wise or fair to allow a superior civilization to be overrun by an inferior one simply because of a slogan about numbers?

It told us that outvoted white women rioted in New Orleans

to keep four six-year-old Negro girls from attending school because old traditions die slowly, and democracy works through
the minds and hearts of the people. And it told us that voteless
Africans rioted in Nyasaland to protest their inclusion in a
Federation run by white men because Africans are still savages
and not fit for self-government.

The same kind of double standard permeates our view of
history too. Warring tribes of Europeans have decimated each
other down through the centuries, but tribal fighting in Somalia
or chaos in the Congo is sufficient excuse to debate the right
of Africans to govern themselves. It took a millennium to en-
trench civil liberties in England—to say nothing of Russia or
Spain—but let there be a wave of arrests in her first decade
and men question whether Ghana should have been given her
independence—as if it were moral or practical in this day and
age for anyone to decide if and when he will "give" such things
to other human beings.

This does not mean that tribal wars or arbitrary arrests
should be condoned in black Africa any more than anywhere
else. Nor does it mean that nothing can be done by the outside
world to help guide new nations over hurdles. What it does
mean is that the inevitability of serious problems provides no
excuse for extending the period of foreign domination over
the objections of the indigenous populations. Even now it is
being said that since South West Africans are not "ready"
for self-government white control would have to be extended
even if there were not the interests of the European community
to consider. By such logic South Africa's failure to provide a
college education for any of her wards in her forty years in
South West Africa becomes good reason to invite her to stay
on for forty years more.

No one maintains that black men are saints. The point is just
the opposite: that they are in fact very human. If they were

less human they would perhaps have learned more from the debauchery and slaughter that have marked the tedious progression of Europe through the centuries, and, having learned more, could avoid more of the hideous miseries that such a progression—even telescoped—will bring to their own continent.

But the strong subconscious predisposition in the white world to view nonwhites as a sort of minority in worth, whose very numbers seem to contribute to the lessening of the value of the individual, gouges ancient scars and fogs up communication to everyone's disadvantage. The recent historical experience of the white man as ruler of the earth is deep in his psyche. And for all his talk about emerging continents and human equality, his stance too often is still that of the inheritor of the earth, now more or less willing to share some of what is his with lesser peoples. Must he also accept *rule* by such peoples? Is it not clear that whites are simply *never* ruled by blacks?

The white man who says of Africa, "This is my home too; I have a right to live here," speaks as it is now the fashion to do. He leaves unuttered what is in any case understood: that the "right" of which he speaks is to live there as top dog. But by what code does anyone have a racial right to be top dog anywhere in the world today? If it be by some code of superior force, does that not invite, and justify, the mustering of a new superior force to dislodge the old whenever possible?

The plain fact is that South Africa is not a white man's country; even less so is South West Africa, where settlers arrived late and stayed on in the guise of the black man's protectors. Sooner or later these facts are going to be ratified, at the polls or on the barricades.

But neither need these places be black man's country if white and black, and those who are neither white nor black, could decide that this was to be the country of all who are willing to live there in equality. And it is also a fact that it is the white man, not the black, who is blocking such a solution, who will not countenance the type of safeguards of individual rights that could be his protection in time to come, were he to need them then as the black man needs them now.

It would be wonderful if a formula could be found by which everyone, regardless of race, could live wherever he wished. But such a formula for Africa can hardly be based on the premise that the white man must run the show, or even that he should have half the legislative seats for one one-hundredth of the population. White men so convinced of their superiority that they would find it unacceptable to live in equality with blacks—to accept the likelihood of a black majority electing a black prime minister, and all the rest of it—should move to a place where a white majority would not present such problems. They may have to accept a far lower standard of living without black labor to draw on, but prejudice can cost, like other luxuries.

Even those Europeans willing, and able in practice, to accept equality as the price for staying in Africa are heirs to the sins of their forebears, and more than likely of their own past. And it may not always be easy to persuade those who have been treated as not quite human that when the pendulum swings they should accord their erstwhile masters the benefit of the doubt about sudden espousals of equality. It is almost beyond belief that there will not be a period of unleashed unreason when the change comes, for it is not the general experience in human affairs that victims of the past can act as if it had never occurred.

If white men in southern Africa understand what it is to say that Africa is their home too, they should long since have turned their energies to minimizing the arduousness of the change in the relationship between the races. There is nothing inherently correct about an African's perspective on history or current affairs or anything else, but if men of widely diverging perspectives are to live together amicably they had best realize quickly just how different their perspectives have come to be. Once this has been done, it may be possible to adjust and then to find understanding.

When Americans bother to think of slavery at all, they think of something Lincoln abolished in 1863. When Africans think of slavery, they are more likely to think of something Western civilization practiced for centuries before that—and still practices, or at any rate condones with slight aesthetic modifications, *at the foot of Africa itself,* today. It is irrelevant that blacks have also practiced slavery—irrevelant not because it is not true, not because it is not as terrible done by blacks as by whites; but irrelevant because it is in no way material to the issue of continuing white dominion over blacks.

Similarly, the magnificent contributions that white men have made to Africa over the centuries will not be preserved by ignoring the toll these same white men have exacted from the land and its people. Most of these contributions were as freighted with greed as they were coated in pious mouthings about higher duties. And if it is senseless for white men to be overwhelmed by feelings of guilt, it is no less senseless for them to act as if the black man's preoccupation with ending white domination is irrational ingratitude.

Men of good will of all races will always work for a world free of race hate and of all other hate. They will pray that the nonwhite majority now coming into its due will react to responsibility with less avarice and more charity than did its predecessors; and will oppose tyranny by men of any color over men of any color. But one hardly makes a promising start toward such goals by first renewing fealty to the primacy of one's skin over one's humanity. How can one go on practicing white racialism even as one goes on insisting that the black man's attitude must be nonracial in return?

Thus, one can demand assurances of future international protection for the rights of white minorities, but such demands would carry more conviction if they were accompanied by as zealous a championing of current rights for nonwhites. And one can hope that when black voters are in the majority they will use all available talent in choosing their governments; but it would be folly not to recognize that after 173 years the white majority in the United States has still to use any of its available nonwhite talent in the national Cabinet. It is hard to picture the American electorate voting a black man into the White House, or a reasonable proportion of black men into the national Congress; and one should not be surprised if similar shortcomings mar the voting habits of people with less experience at self-government that we have had.

There are places where time soothes—where the passing of time is in fact the only real hope for peace. But this is not so in South Africa, where the African has less voice than he had a century ago and where the white man has less inclination to listen to what the African wants to say.

In South Africa time is now an abrasive, a countdown, a dead end. However her problems may finally be resolved, South Africa will need generations for soothing and healing; but before this process can start, time must become the ally of goodwill and rational behavior. There are no quick solutions for South Africa. There are only things that might make slow solutions possible.

The General Assembly of the United Nations has now formally called on its member nations—by a vote of 97 to 2 with 1 abstention—to take "separate and collective action" to bring about the abandonment of South Africa's race policies. It should be clear that such action cannot come too soon.

But it is odd how great the gap between words and deeds seems to be when it comes to acting on the basis of one's own prognoses. Or perhaps the gap is between the saying of something and the believing of it; so that men can issue the direst of predictions and undertake only the most piddling of preventives, as if they did not believe their own prophecies and only wish to be numbered among those who will be able to say "I told you so" if the worst should come to pass. Thus foresight is wasted and unnecessary calamities take place as predicted.

It is a commonplace in South Africa and among those who follow her affairs elsewhere to say that time is running out, to warn against the carnage just ahead, and then to pass on to other matters. In this way even now the urgency is being sapped from the desperate appeals that are reaching the outside world; and farsighted men find their determination to act against South Africa before it is too late diluted by secret hopes that their own predictions will turn out to be wrong.

But if time is running out for South Africa, so is it also running out for America in South Africa. For the machine guns and horsewhips of Sharpeville and Cape Town are no farther from America's jugular than are the jungles of Laos, the firing squads of Havana, or the bridge at Andau.

There was a time not very long ago when the word "America" sang out hope and generosity and compassion, as indeed it still does where the contrast is at hand between American drift and Soviet despotism. But to much of the globe Soviet despotism is still only an American accusation, to be weighed against observed American performance and untested Soviet promises, and against the immediate impact of each on pressing local miseries.

How are men to judge this performance if we go on, in

Michael Scott's memorable phrase, "condemning tyranny in
one part of the world and condoning it on specious procedural
grounds in another"? Or if, in swift succession, we find occasion
to lecture Angolans against the use of violence; to oppose U.N.
resolutions calling for "consideration" of sanctions (i.e., the
only nonviolence that might work) against South Africa; and
to organize and underwrite an invasion of Cuba? And if Castro
in two years had provoked us sufficiently to warrant an announcement after the invasion that our "patience" is not "inex-
haustible," is it unreasonable for many to find a suggestive contrast between this announcement and the fact that several centuries of oppression in southern Africa appear to have fatigued
this "patience" hardly at all?

It is tragic, and may yet be tragedy triplicated, that so often
this kind of American performance leaves an open field to
communist promises. Tragedy first for the people whose agony
is extended by our confusion and myopia. Tragedy next for
Americans who are inviting a debacle that will not spare them
because they were ignorant of its causes and unaware of its
dimensions. Tragedy, finally, for the whole human race, including those who turned against us when we left them nowhere else
to turn, if our failures enable the communists to capture the
world. For then no men, not those who suffered in southern
Africa nor those who caused the suffering nor any others, will
know either peace or freedom.

So it may be said that the fate of continents and coalitions,
and perhaps of generations, hangs in the balance in southern
Africa; and the consciences of great nations sleep now at their
own peril.

I have puzzled over it and am not sure I can explain, even
to myself, the deep and unsettling affection I have come to
have for South Africa. Someone from Mississippi might un-

derstand this sort of affection—someone from Mississippi who
deplores the social system that produced him but who loves
Mississippi for all his disapproval of her habits of life. But then
that would be loving one's home, as one so often loves members
of one's family whose behavior one does not condone.

Something of my feeling for South Africa surely comes of
her natural charms, but I have been to other places with
climate and scenery as admirable and have escaped uncaptured.
One loves places too for people with whom they have been
shared, and what an extraordinary assortment of humanity
shares southern Africa. This is the land where the traveler from
Umtata to Vryheid passes through Port Shepstone and Aman-
zimtoti and Pietermaritzburg and Ladysmith on his way, and
magic seems to inhabit even the names of the most wayward,
lusterless places.

But when all these things have been added together there is
yet something more that enchants the whole far beyond the
sum of its parts. I suspect that what is unique about this country, what grips the emotions beyond landscapes and breezes
and friendships, is the enormity of her misery.

There is much to be said of the grandeur of this wounded,
crying place, of her game parks and her history, of such great
opportunity buried in such great opulence; and it is right that
these things should be said. But there is much that must be
said too about the central, overwhelming fact of her present
condition, and on balance these are the more important things
to say at this time. For this is a place gnashing her teeth and
weeping and bleeding and destroying herself as no other place
in the world, a place of ordinary men turned heroes and of ordinary men going mad. Nowhere else on earth is the lunacy of
man's abuse of himself so grotesquely underlined by visible
evidence of what might otherwise be. And this tragic success
in perverting so much that is so lovely and so promising into

a sleepless nightmare for most of her people commands a compassion, where otherwise might abide simply admiration or envy.

Many are the visitors whom South Africa has afflicted in this same strange way. But these are usually not the visitors who skim her surface and praise her business climate and her rose gardens. For the more you love this land, the more you understand and are held by her, the more you know how harmful is this kind of praise; and those who love her best know all the worst about her, and will speak out not to praise but to protest and to sound alarms. And those who hold the power in this place, who love not South Africa but some mad dream that never was and can never be, will brand them traitors and enemies for sounding such alarms, and jail or deport or ban them. Indeed one wonders what there will be to say in time to come for these people who, when all power was theirs, used it to degrade and torment, and could find not wisdom nor love to soften arrogance.

There is so much of South Africa that I have never seen and that I yearn to see. I have been there only by winter, and then too often in haste or flight. I have missed the sea from the top of Table Mountain, and Pretoria banked in jacarandas for the spring, and the Garden Route in flower. But most of all I have missed seeing this crisp and bountiful child of Nature blessed with the concord that can be the order of human existence where so much is available to all if no one takes what should belong to others.

That is the greatest beauty of all, and that no one has yet seen in South Africa. But those who love her most will work and fight and pray that somehow this will come to pass while they are still around to glory in the wonder of it.

AUTHOR'S NOTE

I am grateful to The Macmillan Company for publishing this book, and especially to my editor, Mr. Peter Ritner. Without his enthusiasm neither publisher nor author would have considered such an undertaking, and without his guidance the author would have been in a constant quandary about how to proceed.

I am of course most deeply indebted to Sherman Bull and Emory Bundy, my companions on the journey to South West Africa. Without their help there would have been nothing to write about, and without their extensive notes and generous assistance it would not have been possible to compile this record with suitable accuracy and thoroughness.

To overwork a paraphrase, rarely have so few owed so much to so many. Perhaps the most humbling of debts is that owed to unknown or briefly-met people who jeopardize their own positions to help strangers. There are many people of all races in South and South West Africa to whom we owe such debts. There are many others whom we never met but to whom we are also deeply indebted, because without their silence about our activities and whereabouts, the police would surely have discovered before we were out of the country that we were the Europeans who had been meeting illegally with Africans. We hope all these people will someday be able to see this book and that they will feel the risks they took were not useless.

A number of South West Africans—notably some tribal

chiefs, a few members of Location Advisory Councils, and scattered leaders of communities like Rehoboth and Hoachanas —have spoken up against the South African Government without regard to the cost to themselves, which often has been considerable. Our indebtedness to such people as the Reverend Markus Kooper, Mr. Hans Beukes, and some of the great chiefs with whom we were able to spend time will become evident in the course of this book. We wish also to express special appreciation to the men who have escaped from South West Africa and have appeared as petitioners at the United Nations in the time since our trip. These men—Mr. Ismael Fortune, Mr. Jacob Kuhangua, Mr. Sam Nujoma, Mr. Uatja Kaukuetu, Mr. Charles Kauraisa, and Mr. Zedekia Ngavirue —have always found time to be helpful to us despite the great burdens they carry as the spokesmen of their people.

Many other South West Africans have, however, felt obliged to conceal their views and to act covertly or not at all. I have tried to protect the anonymity of everyone, both South and South West African, who did not wish his identity to be revealed. To do this it has been necessary to telescope a number of incidents and to obscure dates, localities, and other data whenever such information might help the South African Government identify vulnerable individuals still within its grasp. I believe this has been done without impairing the integrity of the narrative: conditions are reported exactly as we found them, and I have tried to record information and points of view faithfully, even when it has not been possible to provide precise identification of sources.

I have been told of some Americans who have recently been permitted to travel through South West Africa with relatively little official interference. It would be an unexpected blessing if the South African Government as a by-product of our trip and of other recent events were to realize the futility of seeking to maintain an iron curtain around a vast and thinly populated area. But even should such a realization dawn, I suspect it is too much to hope for the repeal of laws which prohibit the free movement of people within the Territory and to places abroad. I fear it will be a long time before border-running and clandestine meetings and sneaking about under pretexts or by dark, have become needless exercises in melodrama in southern Africa. Indeed, I have heard of other Americans who complained that they were confronted with a good deal of official suspicion or hostility, apparently in part because of our activities. We regret any inconvenience we may have caused these travelers, and hope they will realize it is the government that makes such laws, not those who are obliged to ignore them.

Sherman, Emory and I wish to express our gratitude to the Reverend Michael Scott, to Mr. and Mrs. Mburumba Kerina, and to Mr. Jariretundu Fanuel Kozonguizi, who first thought of us in connection with a trip to South West Africa; and to a number of other people who were particularly helpful before, during, and after the trip. The Kerinas and Kozo never seemed to weary of answering our questions. Their briefings were invaluable. So were the annual reports of the United Nations Committee on South West Africa. We commented on these reports when we appeared before the Fourth Committee of the U.N. after our return: "We found time and time again that the South West Africa Committee reports had depicted accurately, and even vividly, complex conditions, an understanding of which seemed to us almost essential to any appreciation of the problems of South West Africans. . . . It seemed almost a miracle that a group working at such a distance and under such handicaps could have amassed so great a wealth of detailed, accurate information and could then have compiled this information with such fairness, courage, and judgment."

The Continental Travel Bureau of Chapel Hill, North Carolina, was helpful far beyond the call of normal professional services. Professor James W. Angell of Columbia University, Miss Pat Baillargeon, Mrs. Beth Brod, Miss Cynthia Courtney, Miss Lois Demone, Miss Jean Fairfax, Mr. Joel L. Fleishman, Mr. Tad Foote, Mr. William Forgie, Mr. Sidney Gerber, Miss Alice Gilbert, Miss Mary Gilson, my very dear aunt, Mrs. Ruth Goldberg, Mr. James T. Harris, Jr., Mr. Fred Jarvis, the Reverend and Mrs. Charles M. Jones, Mr. Thomas O. Jones, Mr. Nick Kangas, Mrs. Hortense King, Mr. Philip Leahy, Mr. Ralph Menapace, Mr. Merrill Miller, Mr. Henry Neale, Miss Elizabeth Parker, Mr. and Mrs. Seif Patwa, Mr. John McC. Phillips, Miss Ann Queen, Dean Aura E. Severinghaus of the College of Physicians and Surgeons of Columbia University, Mr. Alex Shakow, Mr. Pete Sinclair and Mr. Kurt Wehbring all went out of their way to facilitate preparations for the trip or to ease difficulties that arose before our efforts in connection with it were completed. We are indeed grateful to each of these people, and to Steb, Nancy, and Sam Bowles, three of the dearest and most delightful friends who have ever cheered a returning traveler.

Mr. Adlai Hardin, Jr. and Mr. Bill Boyd added immeasurably to my first visit in South Africa, and the hospitality and friendship of many South Africans added immeasurably to both visits. Some of these South Africans I shall not name because they knew of my political activities, and some I shall not name because they did not know of these activities; but I wish to express here my appreciation to them all.

I am also grateful to Senator Hubert Humphrey for his patience and graciousness when I had to leave his staff at a moment that found all hands already overtaxed; and to Miss Betty Goetz, Mrs. Mabel Snyder, Mrs. Rosa Nichols and Mrs. Evelyn Elmore of Senator Humphrey's staff, parts of whose

offices it was my good luck to share. Without the help of these
ladies I could never have wound things up in time to make the
necessary arrangements for the trip.

Additionally, my heartfelt thanks go to Mr. Roger Baldwin,
Mr. and Mrs. Walter Brundage, Dr. Prynce Hopkins, Mr. and
Mrs. F. David Lapham, Mrs. Dorothy Schiff, and to the delegates of the 11th Congress of the United States National Student Association, for financial assistance at critical moments;
to the Reverend Fred Boynton for preparing the tape recordings for presentation to the Fourth Committee; and to Mr.
N. Pilar, Dr. Enrique Rodriguez Fabregat, and many other
distinguished representatives of African, Asian, Latin, and
Scandinavian nations at the U.N., whose kindnesses and coun-
sel made our inexperience and ineptness less of a burden than
would have seemed possible in advance. We are particularly
grateful to a great lady from Liberia, Dr. Angie Brooks, who
has made heroic efforts on behalf of South West Africa at the
U.N., and who took upon herself the additional chore of seeking to set the record straight about us as individuals.

Many people extended themselves to help us tell about what
we had seen in South West. Some of these, like Miss Vernie
Wolfsberg and Mrs. C. A. Nickoloff of the Minnesota Association for the United Nations, and Mr. Jim Reese, then president of the student body at the University of Minnesota, went
to a great deal of trouble to arrange speaking trips. I am particularly indebted to Mrs. Ruth Hagy Brod of *College News
Conference* and to Mr. Ben Wechsler of Cleveland, who gave
unstintingly of their time and knowledge to bring the situation
to the attention of the general public via newspapers and TV.

Above all, there are our families, without whose understanding and assistance the trip would have been impossible. Mary
Bundy, Emory's wife, insisted that he not be excluded on her
account, and supported herself and their infant daughter dur-

ing his absence. His younger brother John, and Mary Bundy's sister and brother-in-law, Mr. and Mrs. James Thwing, were uniquely generous with time and money. A special word should be said about Sherman's wife Marcia, and about his mother and his sister Vida; their great spirit made it possible for him to carry on after the sudden tragic death of his father. My own parents never failed to find ways to help us overcome difficulties, no matter what the inconvenience to themselves; and a host of other relatives—especially my brother Larry and his wife, and my sister, Mrs. Dorothy Bloch—provided encouragement and affection that can never be forgotten. There are no words to convey what is felt for families like these.

A great many people have assisted in one way or another with the preparation of this book or with the presentation of other materials concerned with our findings in South West Africa. I should like particularly to thank Mr. Patrick Arton, Mr. Lewis Nkosi, Mr. Jolyon Nuttall, and Dr. and Mrs. Leslie I. Rubin, among other South Africans; and Mr. Gary Bellow, Mr. Jim Benenson, Mr. and Mrs. Lowell P. Beveridge, Jr., Mr. and Mrs. John Boettiger, Miss Marcia Borie, Miss Sarah Collins, Dr. and Mrs. William Craig, Mrs. Winifred Courtney, Dr. John Davis, Mr. Eli Evans, Mrs. Ann Feldman, Miss Kay Folger, Miss Sylvia Grossman, Mr. Percy E. Haley, Mr. John Harris, Mr. William Johnston, Mr. and Mrs. Paul Jones, Mr. Peter Lapham, Mr. Stephen Lee, Mr. Jim MacArthur, Mrs. Marge MacNamara, Mrs. Edith Marks, Miss Leah Marks, Mrs. Sue Mellins, Mr. Dave Metcalf, Miss Anne Morrison, Mrs. Barbara Palmore, Mrs. Leslie Perrin, Mr. Lee Price, Mr. Harlan Robinson, Ensign Frank Roosevelt, Mr. and Mrs. D. Piel, Miss Jane Symonds and the staff of the Africa Bureau in London, Mme. Anne-Marie Stokes, Mr. Gore Vidal, Mr. and Mrs. Harry West, and Miss Joyce Weissman. Miss Maureen Corr and Mrs. Daisy Lippner were always kind and effi-